THE DESIGN OF FEAR

An Artist's Hauntings and Creations,
from Walt Disney World's
Haunted Mansion and Beyond

RJ Ogren

Theme Park Press
www.ThemeParkPress.com

© 2016 RJ Ogren

No part of this publication may be reproduced, distributed, or transmitted in any form or by any means, including photocopying, recording, or other electronic or mechanical methods, without the prior written permission of the publisher, except for brief quotations embodied in critical reviews and certain other noncommercial uses permitted by copyright law.

Although every precaution has been taken to verify the accuracy of the information contained herein, no responsibility is assumed for any errors or omissions, and no liability is assumed for damages that may result from the use of this information.

Theme Park Press is not associated
with the Walt Disney Company.

The views expressed in this book are those
of the author and do not necessarily reflect
the views of Theme Park Press.

Theme Park Press publishes its books in a variety of print and electronic formats. Some content that appears in one format may not appear in another.

Editor: Bob McLain
Layout: Artisanal Text

ISBN 978-1-68390-018-4
Printed in the United States of America

Theme Park Press | www.ThemeParkPress.com
Address queries to bob@themeparkpress.com

To my wife and best friend, Suzanne

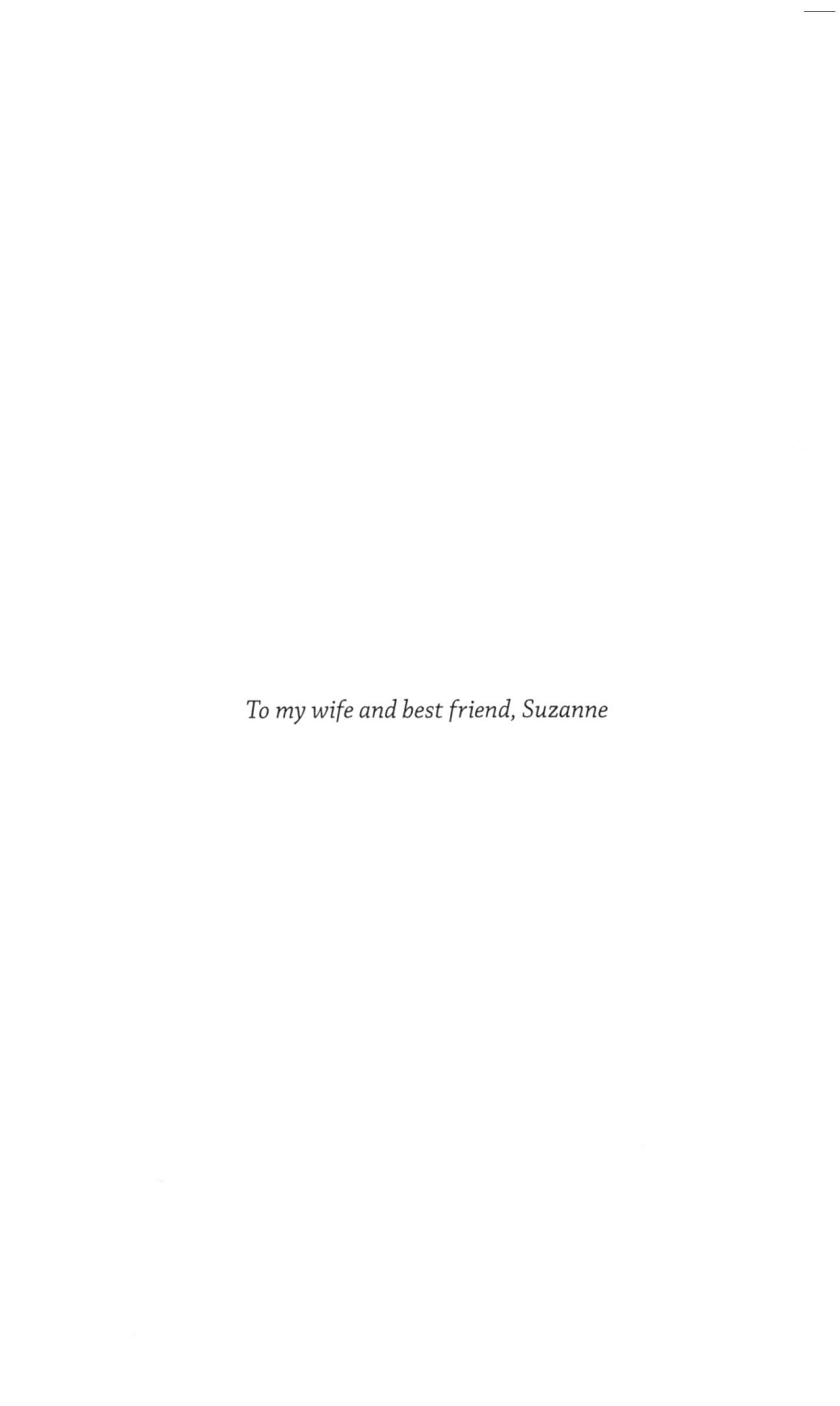

Contents

1	Something Wicked Is Here	1
2	I Started Life in a Fireplace	5
3	Screams, Groans, and Moans	11
4	And Then a Dwarf Called	23
5	An Optical Delusion	29
6	Blood Red Hand	37
7	The Dog Saw It—Ask Rascal!	41
8	Selling Myself in Chicago	47
9	Sonny Acres	51
10	Scream Zone	57
11	Into the Jaws of a Clown	69
12	We Really Are in HELL!	77
13	The *Queen* in Long Beach	83
14	In a Walnut Grove	89
15	Hallucinations—and Fantasy	93
16	Hey, Fred, Bring a Hammer!	103
17	Back and Forth on the I-5	107
18	Pissed-off Parrots	117
19	I Do Believe in Ghosts	127
20	Work, Work, Work—And Then Fun	133
21	The Maw	141
22	...And Beyond	145
	Acknowledgments	153
	About the Author	155
	More Books from Theme Park Press	157

CHAPTER 1
SOMETHING WICKED IS HERE

Pitch black—no moon—and something just brushed past my ankle.

"Try it again," said Brad.

Ignoring him, I kicked with my feet, hoping to frighten whatever had touched me.

"Try it again." I didn't reply, so Brad asked, "What's wrong?"

"Nothing." I turned on the flashlight that dangled from my belt, and aimed the beam downward. Seeing nothing, and breathing a sigh of relief, I turned off the flashlight, as I repeated, "Nothing." The flashlight had made me night blind, so I said, "Wait a second. I need to let my eyes adjust to the darkness and the black light."

My assistant Brad and I were in the middle of the woods, on a farm west of Chicago. We were in the process of installing a gigantic monster figure, to surprise guests on a Halloween haunted hayride. The claws of this creature would extend outward, above the heads of the guests and appear to reach for them.

The monster had a four-foot tall skeleton-like head and eight-foot long segmented arms, with bony hands and claws for fingernails. A wispy, gray cloth covered the figure.

This "thing" was suspended above me, in a huge oak tree, and I was standing on a five-foot high platform. I grabbed the one-inch square aluminum bars attached to the arms and pushed outward, causing the glowing figure to extend over the dirt path for the hayride. This would be how the operator (puppeteer) would maneuver the creature over a hay wagon when it drove by. The puppeteer could move the hands and arms up and down, or left and right—if it worked properly. It had worked in my studio in Virginia when we first built it.

I could just make out Brad on the ground; the gray stripes on his black shirt emitted a soft glow. "Perfect!" I yelled to him.

"Yeah, except it needs to be a bit higher. Not a good idea to take out a guest in a wagon."

"Rats! You're right. That would really scare them though ... RATS!!!" I yelled louder. "Damn! Something is up here on the platform. It just brushed my leg—again!" The hair stood up on the back of my neck. I had visions of something with red eyes biting my ankle. Quickly retracting the monster's arms, I began jumping around on the platform, hoping to scare away whatever this wicked thing was.

Brad turned on his flashlight and aimed it at my feet.

"See anything?" I yelled down to him.

"Yeah."

"Wha ... what?"

"A black cat."

"Oh, great! Really?!"

Brad laughed. "Yeah, right there." He pointed with the flashlight beam, and I looked over to see a black cat sitting near the corner of the platform staring at me—with yellow eyes, and greeting me with a soft "meow." Then, the feline calmly came over and rubbed against my leg.

As my heart rate slowed, I said, "Meow to you—you, you...."

Brad laughed again. "Does everything scare you?"

"No," I laughed with him. "Just some things."

"Such as?"

"You're enjoying this, aren't you?"

"Oh, yeah." Brad said. "So, what does scare you?"

"You really want to know?" He nodded. "Okay: darkness, rats, spiders, snakes, zombies…."

"Zombies?"

"Yeah, zombies! Also horror movies, and giant ants."

"I thought you liked horror movies."

"I do."

"You're very strange." Long pause. The cat continued rubbing against my leg, and meowing. Then Brad laughed again.

"What now?" I asked.

"Giant ants?"

"Yes … giant ants. And chimneys."

"Oh, come on! Now you're messin' with me!"

"Not really."

CHAPTER 2
I STARTED LIFE IN A FIREPLACE

The sky was dark and gray. Rain spattered my face as I ran for my life. I knew they were coming. I ran faster.

The bridge over the Mississippi River seemed to go on forever. A foreboding structure, yet it offered me no protection. I needed to get to a safe place. I looked over my left shoulder and scanned the sky for *them*.

Giant ants!

My legs ached as I ran toward the end of the bridge and the entrance to the Rock Island, Illinois, arsenal. The army would protect me. If I could just get to the WWII tank at the museum, I could hide inside.

The rain came down in buckets, partially obscuring the surprised and concerned faces of the people I passed. Suddenly, a familiar face caught my eye. It appeared behind the windshield of a white car that came toward me ... and continued past me.

My mother.

I ran even faster.

I knew she'd have to drive all the way across the Centennial Bridge to Davenport, Iowa, before she could turn around. She couldn't stop on the bridge. I reached the Illinois side of the bridge and stopped to wait for her to come back. If I ran into the arsenal grounds, she wouldn't know where to look for me.

I was doomed. A soaking rat. All hell was going to break out at any moment. I would be caught ... by ants or by my mother.

The white car pulled up beside me. My trembling hand opened the passenger door, and I flopped into the seat. At least I was safe from the ants.

"Don't get the seat wet!" I still wasn't safe from my mother.

Breathing hard and shaking, I sat there in silence. A drowned, ten-year-old ... rat. I was numb. Wait a minute! Did my mother just tell me not to get the seats wet? Oh, right. It's my mother. She always said things like this. I stifled a giggle.

She glared at me as she drove away from the curb. "Why didn't you wait for me in front of the theater?"

"I ... movie ended an hour ago...." I gulped. "So, when you didn't show up ... I started walking. Then, it got dark and stormy, so I ran!"

"You ran?"

A long pause, then, "From them."

"What? Who is *them*?"

Another long pause, then, "The giant ants."

She gave me a quizzical look. "The ants?" she said, her voice trailing off, then silence. *Uh oh, here it comes*, I thought. She exploded. "The movie?! Giant ants?! Is that what *Them* is about?!"

"Uh, huh." I wished I could crawl deeper into my seat.

"That's it! No more horror movies for you!"

My voice trembled, "But, Mom ... I loved the movie!"

She started to say something. Her mouth clamped shut. She stared out the windshield, shook her head, and spoke almost in a whisper, "I should have left you in the fireplace."

"What?" I was stunned. I knew when to keep my mouth shut, BUT, *in the fireplace?!*

A FIREPLACE?!

We reached the driveway of our big, two-story house on 21st Street in Rock Island. I was almost in tears as I climbed out of the car. The rain had stopped.

My mother yelled at me as I ran to the steps of our front porch, "Get some rags and clean the car seat before you get out of those wet clothes!"

Entering the living room, I stopped to stare at the fireplace. I gulped. I knew I needed to talk to my dad. And soon.

It was 1954. I had just turned ten. Lots of things I liked could also scare me or give me nightmares. And my mom hated that.

My dad, Daniel, was an easy-going, lovable man. When I related this *Them* incident to him, he thought it amusing. We were seated in the living room, beside the fireplace. My mom, Evelyn, could be heard in the kitchen, banging pots, pans, and dishes. She was still mad at me, even though she was the one who had forgotten to pick me up!

"Your mother is upset."

"Sorry, Dad. It was ... I mean...."

"Look, sport." He always called me *sport*. "I know you like scary movies and radio shows. But you always have nightmares, which upset her. She doesn't understand why you would want to watch or listen to these shows if they scare you. You also buy scary comic books, some in 3-D."

"Sorry." I sank lower into the big chair I was sitting in. Was he going to tell me I couldn't do any of that anymore?

"I'm not going to ask you to stop, but ... well, here's an idea. After you watch or read something scary, find something funny to watch or read, before you go to bed."

I almost smiled. There was hope for me yet. "Okay, Dad. I'll go read some funny comic books now, so I won't have nightmares about *Them*.

My dad laughed, and said, "Running across the bridge, being chased by giant ants *is funny*!" He got out of his chair and patted me on the shoulder. "Look, sport, a lot of things will scare you in life. Run upstairs to your room and read. I'll talk to your mother."

"Okay, thanks Dad." As I got up to leave the room, I spotted the fireplace. "Dad?"

"Yes, sport?"

"Could I ask you something?"

"Sure."

I sat back down—next to the fireplace.

"Mom said today that she should have left me in the fireplace." I gulped, because I had a mental picture of the witch in "Hansel and Gretel."

Dad suppressed a smile as he explained her remark. "When I was discharged from the navy, soon after the end of World War II, your mom and I couldn't find a house or apartment to rent. Landlords refused to rent to vets, if they had kids."

"What?"

"Let me finish. As it turned out, the city of St. Charles, where we were at the time, let us stay in the clubhouse next to the city pool and golf course."

"In Potawatomi Park?" I remembered that park, and loved it, and its Indian name.

"Yes. We were there for the winter. We didn't need to light the big fireplace—we had an electric heater—and your mother thought the fireplace was a great spot, out of the way, where you could sleep. She blocked the fireplace opening, so you wouldn't roll out."

"I slept in the fireplace?!" My dad nodded. "Boy, am I glad Mom didn't light a fire!"

"Me, too," he added, smiling again.

"How long were we there?"

"Just a few months. Your mother got frustrated because we couldn't find a permanent place to live. She finally went to the Aurora newspaper and placed an ad, seeking an apartment for all of us, saying she would drown her children if necessary."

I was appalled. "What? Really? Did she mean it?"

"No, of course not." I was quite convinced of his sincerity—knowing my mom. "But the ad editor told the news editor, and your mom and your three-year-old brother ended up with our pictures on the front page, with a story about vets with kids unable to rent housing."

"What a cool story! What happened?"

"It worked. The story caught on everywhere, and the landlords began to rent to them."

"Wow! That is really...."

My dad interrupted me. "Yeah, so, see. You basically started your life in a fireplace."

"Right. But, Dad, why would Mom want to leave me there?"

Dad smiled and cleared his throat. "She didn't mean it. She was just frustrated with you."

I thought for a moment before saying, "Remind me never to frustrate her again."

"Probably a good idea."

"Hey, Dad! Maybe that's why I'm afraid of cobwebs and spiders."

"What do you mean?"

"Well, you see cobwebs and spiders in fireplaces."

His eyes had a twinkle in them as he replied, "Well, you never know."

CHAPTER 3
SCREAMS, GROANS, AND MOANS

"Who's there?"

The moaning was loud, and close by. I stood up and looked over the top of a tombstone. Nothing.

"All right. Good joke. Lee? Tom? A withered head popped up beside me. I jumped. Screams, groans, and moans filled the cemetery.

Music. Singing. Ghosts moving all around me. Now I laughed. What was there to be afraid of? I was working in the Haunted Mansion at Walt Disney World. But then … the loud moan came again, this time behind me and louder than the usual cacophony of groans and eerie music I was accustomed to in this attraction.

I turned around and stepped toward the back of the cemetery, careful not to fall through openings in the ground area. A lone, glowing figure suddenly lunged from behind the hearse in the scene. "Ooowooo!" I jumped, then laughed as the figure laughed, too.

"Hi, Randy!"

"Cute!"

"I *did* scare you, didn't I?"

"All right. I admit it. It was good moaning."

Jeff smiled. His Maintenance work shirt glowed in the black light. "I love working in this place," he said. Jeff worked the third shift at night, in the Haunted Mansion.

I looked around. The singing busts were harmonizing the "Grim Grinning Ghosts" song. "Yeah, me too." Just beyond the busts, I could see the opera singer figure creating her own solo moment, and, above the opening leading to the cemetery, the creepy eyes of the black raven stared at me. I looked back at Jeff and asked, "Hey, what time is it?"

"6:30. Almost time to clock out for me. Going home to sleep, then put up the Halloween decorations."

"You'd better hurry. Halloween is tomorrow," I reminded him.

He laughed. "I just put a carved pumpkin on our porch." He smiled, and his teeth glowed yellow because of the ultraviolet lighting. "I suppose you put up all kinds of decorations."

"Yeah. We have our own little Haunted Mansion."

I said goodbye to Jeff and walked through the graveyard, stopping to inspect ghosts and props. Each morning, I, along with Lee, Tom, and Jayne, would leave the Animation Art Studio, located behind It's a Small World, and check different attractions for any repairs that might be needed. Some were quick fixes that we could do immediately, but if a figure needed a new skin, for example, we would instruct Maintenance to pull that figure and bring it to our studio.

WDW's Haunted Mansion is where I perfected my techniques of working with black light, low-level lighting, and darkness. As you ride through that attraction in a Doom Buggy, the changes in lighting create more interest, and constantly affect the irises of your eyes. Some of the Haunted Mansion's special effects, like the Grand Ballroom scene or the Hitchhiking Ghosts in the mirrors, are based on classic magic tricks. Every time I work on a haunted house, hayride, or other Halloween venue, I think about the mansion and use what I learned there to create scares.

It's time for you to "walk" through the mansion with me; experience the effects, the ghosts, the changing light levels, and stopping, at times, to check figures or props

... or just to enjoy the moment. So, let's go back to 1970's Walt Disney World.

I open the huge, wooden doors, and enter the low-lit parlor. I check the wallpaper for any damage by guests. If a piece has been scraped or pulled off, I mix colors from my paints so I can match the design and colors of the existing wallpaper to repair the damage. I look at the framed painting over the mantel between the doors that lead to the twin stretching rooms. The man in the painting ages and turns into a skeleton in seconds.

Next, I enter a stretching room and close the door. Four large paintings hang on the walls, above where the guests will stand. As the room stretches (many guests think they are in an elevator going down, when, in actuality, it is the wall stretching upward), the paintings lengthen, revealing the comical "deaths" of the subjects on the canvas. The artwork for these paintings was created by Marc Davis, a legendary Disney artist and animator, and one of our bosses from the Disney Studio. Because the paintings are on a roll, like a window shade, they can tear if anything is slightly off kilter. Luckily, this is a rare occurrence, but, if it happens, we can repair and repaint the damaged area. In four years, we've only had to replace two stretch paintings.

A dismembered voice is heard, stating that the chamber we're standing in has no windows and no doors—but! He further says that "there's always my way." Suddenly, the lights go out. It's pitch dark. Lightning strikes at the top of the high ceiling, there is a thunder crack and a scream, as I view a body hanging from the rafters above.

Everything in here looks okay. Good. Don't want to go up there. Only had to do it once. Working on that body means climbing up to the attic of the mansion and leaning out over the stretch room to pull the figure up, then clean it, check it, repair any damage, and lower it down again. Very dangerous; one slip and I could fall through the painted scrim to the floor below, roughly twenty-five feet! Ouch! I do the same checks in the second stretch room; all appears okay there as well.

Having two alternating rooms allows for more guests being moved in a steady flow to the loading area, where you board your Doom Buggy. (By the way, to avoid a long wait time at this attraction, get to it when the park first opens, just before park close, or during the times when a parade is in progress. Another fun tip: when you enter the stretching room, try to stand under the portrait of the young woman holding the parasol and stay there, because that is where the Ghost Host will open the sliding door that leads to the loading area.)

I love the sounds as I walk through the loading area. The attractions are always turned on long before the guests arrive, so that checks can be made to be certain everything is working properly. The Doom Buggies are stopped, awaiting their first passengers. I walk safely between them and onto the stairs leading to blackness. Huge, multi-colored, black-light spiders twitch on over-sized, glowing webs. Lee, Tom, and I paint these in our studio black-light room, trying to outdo each other with the ugliest, scariest creation! (Note: these spiders are long gone now, replaced by incredible, glowing, moving staircases. The experience is like being in an Escher painting—wonderful effect!)

The suit of armor and the endless hallway come into view on my right. The lighting is now low-level regular light. Looking at the suit of armor, I do a double-take and laugh. A cigarette dangles from the armor faceplate. A cast member, possibly Jeff, has left a little joke. I remove the cigarette, wrap it in paper, and put it in my art knapsack.

Next stop is the coffin. The emaciated corpse inside is trying to get out; one bony hand grabbing the lid and pushing it up and down. Hands looks good. A few weeks ago, someone had managed to break off one of his fingers. I had to make a new finger and paint it to match the hand.

I never found the missing finger. Whoever broke it probably took it as a souvenir.

I walk past the hallway doors, with knocker knocking, groans groaning, and doors bulging. I check the grandfather clock, the hands of which rotate backward. We are still in regular, low light here and my eyes have adjusted to it. A few more steps, and we're back in the darkness and black light.

Guests ride their Doom Buggies around this horseshoe-shaped room as they view Madame Leota's talking head inside a crystal ball. Musical instruments dance in the air above the guests, as discordant music plays. The lines holding these instruments are normally invisible, but dust has gathered on them, so they can be seen as dull grey attachments. I make a mental note to call Custodial. They will clean the support lines after the attraction closes. I look at Madame Leota and say, "Hi!" She ignores me.

Leota Toombs—another artist from the Disney Studio, known for her sculpture and painting of numerous Disney figures—was filmed for this projection in the crystal ball. She came to Walt Disney World in the early 1970's, to train the other three artists. When it came time for her to return to the California studio, I was the fortunate artist chosen to take her place at WDW, in the Animation (Audio-Animatronic) Studio, located behind It's a Small World.

The illusion in the crystal ball was created by projecting Leota's filmed image onto a molded head form, similar to a form used to hold wigs. The form had to have molded features: indented eye areas, a nose, etc., so that the projected film loop on the form would appear real. If the form was flat, the face would look as if her features were smashed onto a flat surface.

There are some guests, unfortunately, who think they can jump out of their Doom Buggy to steal something inside the attraction. What they don't realize is that there are sensors, and other devices, that immediately alert the attraction hosts (by means of monitors). The Doom Buggy movement is halted, and a recorded voice requests that you remain in your seat until the ride resumes.

Three occurrences can cause this, or any other attraction, to stop. The first I've just told you about. The other two are safety issues, one when a wheelchair guest is being loaded or unloaded, and the other is when a guest is too slow to enter or exit their Buggy, or if they should fall as they try to get seated or are exiting the attraction.

I was told that, before I began working at WDW, a misguided guest got out of his Doom Buggy and climbed over a railing in an attempt to steal something—and fell through an opening to the basement below, fracturing his leg in the process. His screams and moans could not be heard above those of the other 999 ghostly sounds. He was eventually located and handled by paramedics. I can't verify whether that story is true, since I wasn't there, but it's a good lesson about remaining in your vehicle as instructed.

I look closely at Leota and her crystal ball, to make sure there are no problems. Not long ago, the crystal ball was shattered, by one of those misguided guests, resulting in a new one being made by an aircraft company. It has never worked as well as the original. The projector's light reflection was never seen on the original ball, but on the replacement, a light spot appears on the front of the crystal ball. It ruins the effect, I think.

I must return to the present to tell you more about Leota (the figure and the woman). With the advent of digital imagery, a "new Leota talking head" has replaced the one I worked on. Since Leota Toombs sadly is no longer living, someone else posed and spoke for the new image. It is a masterful re-creation, I must say, and I know Leota would approve. She is still in the Haunted Mansion, however. Leota's small figure image, on the ledge above the guests as they exit the cemetery to the unloading area, calls down, "Come ba-a-a-c-k!" She posed for that, and it is her voice you hear. As a final tribute to her artistry, a tombstone bearing her name is just to the left of the main entrance to the mansion.

I was privileged to know and work with Leota Toombs. About two years after I "took her place" at WDW, she returned and spent three weeks with us, as she worked on new façade artwork for the Polynesian Village Resort. We spent many mornings with her, at breakfast, and she even accompanied us on some of our work sessions. I learned from her, and certainly enjoyed all of her Disney stories. You can read more about those moments in *Together in the Dream*, a book that I co-wrote with my wife, Suzanne, who was also a cast member at Walt Disney World. I always think of Leota whenever I visit the Haunted Mansion.

Time to continue our walk through the attraction.

I leave the black-light Leota room and enter the regular-light Grand Ballroom. Here, ghosts fly in and out of windows and doors, while others celebrate at a birthday party. Another ghost plays a large pipe organ while party guests dance and twirl. Two large paintings hang side by side on a far wall, and the portraits of two ghostly men turn toward each other and fire pistols, as in a duel. There are even ghosts perched on a high chandelier. I check the glass that separates the guests from the ballroom, to make sure there are no holes or scratch marks that would ruin the effect. The images that guests see are reflections of forms underneath where the Doom Buggies ride, and above them as well. In fact, if you lean forward in your Doom Buggy, and look up, you can see the real feet of the chandelier ghosts. The entire room is based on a very old magic trick called Pepper's Ghost.

I go both upstairs and down to check the "real" ghosts. Upstairs, through a hidden door, I enter a black room: black walls and black duvetyn stage curtains. The only items lit are the grey-toned ghosts; shades of grey, painted on fiberglass faces, legs, arms, and hands. The clothing, wigs, and hats are in the same grey shades. Everything looks good. No broken parts. The chandelier ghosts sit on the ledge of the overhang the guests ride under. I am careful as I check them because I could slip and fall twenty feet to a concrete floor. I also have to be mindful of the flying ghosts, going around in circles as if on a merry-go-round.

Back to the hidden door, and down the stairs to the main floor. Another black room, this one inhabited by the birthday ghosts, dancing ghosts, and the ghost playing the organ. Careful not to get hit by the dancers, I approach the ghost who leans forward from her chair to blow out the candles on the cake. She is seated in a black chair, at a black table, both of which perfectly match the height and proportions of the real chair and table in the ballroom. The Doom Buggy cars are passing above me as I look at the lit Grand Ballroom. I can see my reflection next to the birthday ghost. I wave. It looks like I'm in the ballroom, standing right behind her chair. Luckily, there are no guests in the buggy cars to see me! What a great illusion, created by Walt Disney, Marc Davis, and the Imagineers.

Once I check all the figures, I return to the Doom Buggy level, and proceed to the dimly lit attic. My eyes, again, have to adjust to the changing light level.

A ghost suddenly pops up beside me. I jump, then laugh. I've just been scared by one of the pop-up ghosts that artist Harry Holt and I painted in the studio. Harry worked on such animated classics as *Lady and the Tramp*. He created these pop-ups to add to the mansion fun, and he and I spent a week painting them both in UV lighting (for the cemetery) and in regular light for the attic.

Bats fly around in the semi-dark attic. They are actually on a thin, wire frame—like a mobile—which revolves and bounces, making the bats appear to flutter. I only had to make new bats once, because, suddenly, some went missing—which meant either a cast member or a guest took them.

Screams, Groans, and Moans 19

The heart of the bride ghost is thumping away as I walk past her on my way into the cemetery. Walking down the ramp, I stop to look up at the raven in the tree. He looks good, so I continue to the bottom of the ramp to check the caretaker figure and his emaciated dog. Both figures shake with fear as they look into the ghost-filled graveyard.

I'm back in full black light as I begin checking the figures in the cemetery. These characters include ghosts on bicycles and swings, musicians, singing busts ... wait a minute. Something's wrong here. The projected faces of the singing ghosts on the busts look good in grey tones, but from the neck down, they have a greenish hue that ruins the effect. This is caused by the wrong gels being placed in the stage lights. I make another mental note to stop at the Maintenance shop and tell them to change the gels.

Opposite the busts is a horse-drawn black hearse which has a recurring problem. A small red light inside the hearse creates a creepy mood effect. I look at the hearse. No light. Again. Unfortunately, when it burns out, no one ever thinks to replace it. Another note for Maintenance. All these seemingly small details are important for the look of the show.

Next, I check the mummy in the coffin, the opera singer, the animated skeleton arm sticking out of a mausoleum wall, the hand holding a trowel ... hey! Where's the arm? I'll see Maintenance about that when I'm done.

I wave at the hitchhiking ghosts on my way to the exit, where Leota's form is enticing guests to return. Since I'd recently been up on a ladder, making some minor touch-ups to her, there's no reason to check her again. I keep walking to the guest unloading area. Done. No.

Quickly, I go downstairs to the small room used by Audio-Animatronic Maintenance. Jeff's back is to me, leaning over his work table.

"Hey, guys, where is..." but, before I can finish the sentence, Jeff turns around, pointing the missing skeleton arm at me.

"Looking for this?"

"Yes, I thought it might have been stolen again."

"Nope," Jeff answers. "I was going to drop it off at your studio before heading home."

"Why didn't you tell me about it when I saw you earlier?" I ask.

"More fun to think of you freaking out when you noticed it was missing!"

"Thanks, turkey!"

Jeff and his third shift buddy, Allen, both laugh.

"I can take that."

Jeff says, in a mocking tone, "Make it look pretty for us."

"Right." With the arm under my arm, I head back to the studio.

Coffin hand in Haunted Mansion

Haunted Mansion pop-up ghost

Haunted Mansion Stretching Room

CHAPTER 4
AND THEN A DWARF CALLED

Yes, it was one of the Seven Dwarfs. My wife was one of them at the time, in the Walt Disney World character dwarf unit, portraying Sleepy. One of her "co-dwarfs" had a request—which didn't involve her height OR Disney.

Her real name was Belinda, and she wanted to be a skeleton for several Halloween events, including parties and a dance. She wanted to win the Best Costume award at each, and asked if I could paint a skeleton on black leotards and tights, both front and back.

At that time, there were no Halloween costume stores, no internet. You had to create your own costume if you wanted something unique. Unless a skeleton jumps out at me, or crawls out of the ground, or walks into my kitchen and asks for a cup of coffee, I am not afraid of them. I told Belinda I would be happy to make her into a skeleton, but there was a hitch—which I needed to explain to both Belinda and my wife, Suzanne.

I talked to Suzanne first, and then we called Belinda.

"I can do this for you, but you'll have to be wearing the leotard and tights while I'm painting them, so that all the bones are in the right places on your body." Silence at the other end. "Belinda?"

"Yes."

"Suzanne is going to be here with us, while I'm painting you."

"Oh! Then, sure; let's do it."

Belinda came to our house the next day, a Saturday, around two o'clock in the afternoon. She was attending all of the events that evening, but I was certain I had plenty of time to get her ready for them.

To begin with, we sat in two chairs, facing each other, with Suzanne across the room, taking pictures and talking to us. I had a table beside me which held white and black acrylic paints, artist brushes, rags, water, and make-up (for her face and hands).

My idea, for painting my first live skeleton, was to paint the bones first with white, then mix gray for shading the bones to make them look three-dimensional. To my surprise, when I applied the white paint to the upper arm of the leotard, with the brush, then rubbed it with my finger to smooth it out on the material, it turned gray as it soaked in. I stared at it.

"What's wrong?" Belinda asked.

"Nothing. I think I'll let this dry, and then go from there." I wanted to sound like I knew what I was doing, but, in truth, this was all an experiment for me. Luckily, the paint dried quickly.

"This feels weird on my skin underneath."

"I should think so ... and I think it's going to get weirder."

"What?" Suzanne and Belinda said, in unison.

"Just kidding!" I said. *I hope I am*, I thought.

I put more white paint on my brush, and applied it to half of the gray bone. It stayed white. Perfect! It looked really good!

"That looks good," Belinda echoed my thought.

"Wow!" Suzanne exclaimed.

"Yeah, see now I'll continue with just white paint. If you paint it on, then rub it and let it almost dry, then paint over that, the white highlight stands out." I said all this with authority, as if I knew the result all along.

Belinda smiled. "This is going to look so cool."

"Yeah, it is," Suzanne agreed.

I don't think, at that moment, that Belinda totally realized what was about to transpire over the next three hours. I painted her arms, her collar bones, and her upper ribs; painting, rubbing, smoothing, painting again. Then I reached her breasts—and I stopped.

Belinda gave me a half smile. "Ahh, ha...."

"You want me to stop?" I asked, concerned for her.

"No, I'm fine. Just didn't think about this." She looked at Suzanne. "Are you okay with this?"

"I'm fine. It's your call, though."

Belinda took a deep breath.

"Okay?" I asked.

"Okay."

As I painted and lightly rubbed her body for the next two hours, I kept asking if she was okay. Sometimes, her reply was a weak, "Uh, huh," but she insisted I continue. She said it was like getting a very slow, full-body massage. Suzanne remarked that she should consider it performance art.

"Done!" I announced, as I finished the back of her left leg.

"Thank God!" Belinda exclaimed, and we all had a good laugh.

I applied make-up to her face and hands, and sprayed her hair. Unfortunately, I didn't have the best white make-up to use, but the final effect came out delightfully creepy, and I had learned some great techniques in blending on material, with brush and fingers.

AND—Belinda won all the contests!

I left WDW in 1980. I would miss doing unusual projects like "painting a life skeleton," and I would always miss working with the other three artists—we'd had a lot of fun. I went out on my own, to create new creatures and scares for other haunted house venues. Disney would always be with me, thanks to everything I'd learned there, working in all the Magic Kingdom attractions.

While at Walt Disney World, I became proficient working in the dark rides, such as Peter Pan's Flight, Snow White's Scary Adventure, Mr. Toad's Wild Ride, and my favorite attraction, The Haunted Mansion.

Anything to do with scary, creepy, eerie, or the supernatural has always intrigued me. From the time I was a kid, I was hooked on classic horror movies: *Abbott & Costello Meet Frankenstein*, *The Wolfman*, *Dracula*, and *The Invisible Man*, among them. Some of my favorite movies and TV shows, as an adult, include *Poltergeist*, *Alien*, *The Mummy*, *Slither*, *The Walking Dead*, and *Grimm*. If it's scary, even funny, and well done, I have to see it!

I knew I had the background, the passion, and some real fears besides, that would combine to provide me the tools to create my own haunted scares for Halloween venues around the USA.

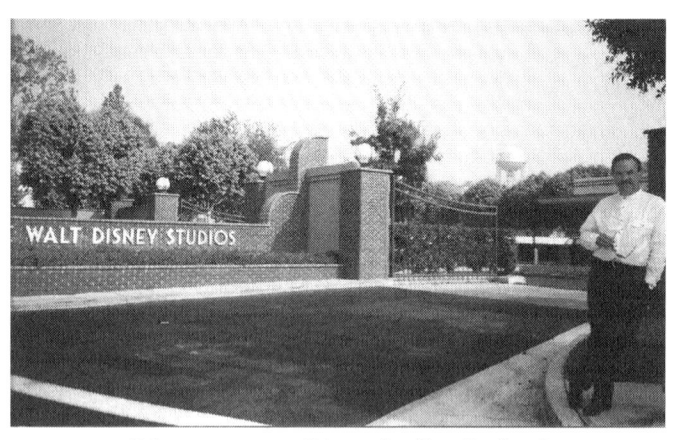

RJ at entrance to Disney Studios, Burbank

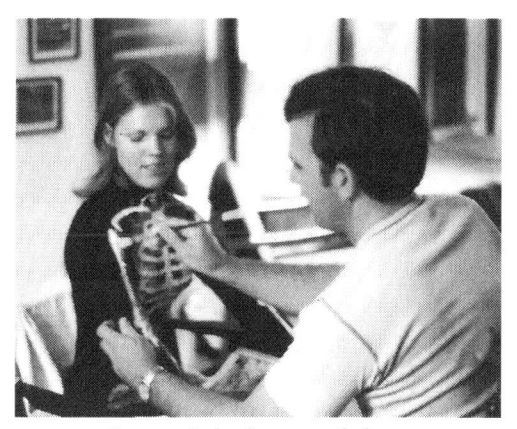

Turning Belinda into a skeleton

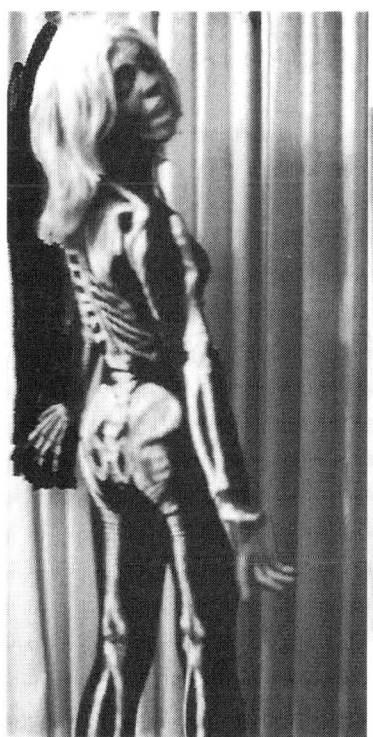

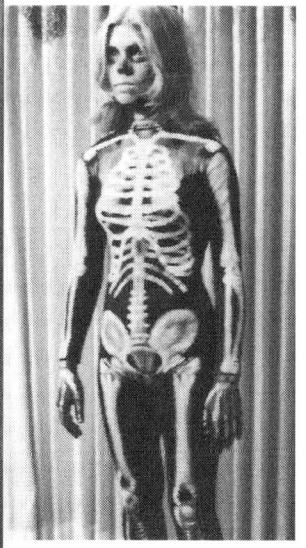

Belinda, completed

CHAPTER 5
AN OPTICAL DELUSION

I looked down at the moonlit river, far below, as it meandered through a valley. I could just make out the sheer cliff walls as they disappeared into inky blackness.

I took a step on the bridge, and had to grab the rope support to steady myself. The bridge swayed from right to left. Some planks in the rope bridge appeared to be either missing or broken—painted by me to look that way. At both ends of the bridge, I viewed the dense green foliage of a forest. Dark. Foreboding. Looking down at the bridge planks, where I'd already painted a black "hole," I envisioned the next thing to paint: a figure of a terrified woman, who had fallen through the hole, and was hanging on to the planks for dear life.

I set my paint, brushes, rags, and water container on the bridge, and kneeled in front of the plywood panel. Any movement, no matter how small, made the bridge move. My first task was to paint the image area with regular latex white paint (it gives off a very dull, dark purple glow in UV lighting). You have to have a white background on which to paint with black-light paint, which requires an undercoat to work properly in UV light

As I finished the white primer coat, a loud voice beside me made me jump.

"When are you going to be done?"

Don't say anything negative. Just smile. It's the owner, and he is paying a large fee for this.

"Oh, hi, John," I said, as I slowly stood up.

"So, when?" he boomed again.

I wondered if he had a hearing problem. He had a bass voice that always bellowed.

His wife, and co-owner of this haunted attraction, stood beside him. She was thin, attractive, and smartly dressed. "Hi, R.J.", she said in a soft voice. She smiled at me.

"Hi, Stephanie."

"This looks beautiful," she said. "And I love the effect."

"Thank you."

John interrupted. "But when will it be done?" His overweight, five-foot, ten-inch frame, and pudgy face, seemed ready to explode.

Come to think of it, he always looks like this. I can never figure out how these two stay together. I answered him in a calm voice: "Not much longer. I have this figure on the bridge and a few others to paint in the forest."

John looked around. "Looks like a lot is left to do."

"Not really." I couldn't quite figure out what he was referring to. "I should be done in just a few days."

"I don't see how. But, get it done. There are other rooms to work on!" He didn't wait for me to reply, as he quickly turned and left the room.

Wow! He is suffering from an optical delusion! I turned to Stephanie. She gave me a smile.

"You're doing great, R.J. Don't let him rattle you. He's like that with everybody. Just keep doing what you're doing. See you soon."

She left, and I looked around the room. What did he mean when he said it looked like I still had a lot to do. I kneeled down and checked the white paint. Totally dry; that was fast. "I wonder if Mr. Blowhard ... no, don't go there."

I went to work, painting the figure. My idea for this woman was that the guests would try to step around, or over her, thinking she was real, and that would cause the bridge to sway even more.

I had suggested to John that he have a costumed employee, all in black, hide in a black area of this large room, and jump out at guests to scare them. John didn't want to pay the additional salary for that, and instead asked me to paint a figure on plywood that his mechanic/electrician could mount on a motor. It would lean out, quickly, from behind a tree or a black wall. This might have worked except that it was mounted on a slow, inadequate motor, with no sound effect, and just moved back and forth, continually. A great scare relies on unexpected surprise on the part of the guest.

This is an argument I have had with more than one owner of a haunted attraction. So many times, they want people in costume, usually bloody, to just stand in full sight, in a room as guests walk through. The zombie or ghoul jumps around, attempting to scare the guest, but the guest has already "seen it coming." Not scary.

I had learned, working at WDW's attractions, that to be effective, different levels of light must constantly affect a guest's eyes as they go through an attraction: low light, black light, strobe light, colored lights, or total darkness.

Think of an everyday experience. It's the middle of the night. You get up out of bed and go to the bathroom. You can see as you make your way because your eyes are adjusted for the darkness. Turn on the bathroom light—Ow! Bright! You squint. Your eyes adjust slowly. When you leave the bathroom, turning out the light, you suddenly can't see anything! This is what the guest experience should be, in a haunted attraction, in order to enjoy it to the fullest.

So, back to the figure on the bridge. I was happy with the woman figure when I finished. She looked as if she would fall to her death if she lost her grip on the bridge planks, plummeting a thousand feet or more into total darkness. In reality, the bridge was only two feet off the floor.

Something small ran across the floor below me, its feet making small clicking sounds. The hairs on the back of my neck stood out. I looked, but saw nothing. *I will stay on the bridge awhile longer. Wish I had my flashlight. Maybe I could reach the worklight switch—no, I'd have to step off the bridge to the floor where "it" is lurking!*

I'm not afraid of the dark. I'm afraid of what's *in the dark*. I thought of the flashlight again. Normally, I didn't use one because it would affect my eyes when I was painting in UV light. Then I thought of something more terrifying: what if I did have the flashlight, turned it on to scan the room, looking for the skittering "it"—and I found it! BUT! All I would see would be two beady eyes, glowing in the flashlight beam. And staring at me! Evil. Deadly. Again, the hair rose on the back of my neck.

Decision. I'll stay on the bridge awhile longer. I heard "it" run across the room again! New decision. Run to the worklight switch. I stepped off the swaying bridge and hurried to the wall—damn! The switch is on the other wall!

I ran into the next room, and bumped into a hanging ghoul. Not as scary. I knew what that was. I hurried to the emergency exit door, and burst out into the Florida sunshine. Yay! The door closed slowly. Nothing followed me out.

I must have looked like a frightened madman, but, as I looked around, I didn't see anyone else. Whew! I walked around the building, and went back in through the main entrance.

"Hi, R.J." It was Frank, the engineer/electrician, walking up on my right. He was smiling—he was always smiling; it seemed fake to me. "I thought you were painting in the forest."

"I was. I am. Just needed a break."

Still smiling, he said, "Oh, okay." I watched him walk away. That's a very strange man, I thought. Creepy, as if he had a slimy secret.

I saw Ed, the elderly maintenance and construction worker, across the lobby. "Hey, Ed," I called out, as I walked over to him.

"Hi," said, Ed, smiling. He wasn't creepy. His smile was genuine. I liked Ed. "You look like you've seen a ghost."

"Yeah. Sort of. Something small. Least I hope it's small. It's running around in the forest room. It scared the crap out of me! Would you mind coming with me, to check it out?"

"Sure. You okay?"

"Yeah."

"Flashbacks?"

"Yeah."

"Understood." Ed was a Korean war vet. I'd been in Vietnam. He understood.

We turned on the worklights as we entered the forest room. Nothing.

"You okay?" Ed asked.

"Yeah, thanks. I am now. Whatever it was is obviously gone—I hope."

"Probably in the next room," Ed said and laughed.

"Yeah, thanks a lot. Now I won't be able to go in the next room."

"Want me to stay here with you?"

"What? And hold my hand? No, I'm fine."

"Okay," Ed said as he walked out. "Just scream if you need me." He turned out the worklights as he left.

I wished I could work with them on, but black-light painting must be done in the dark with only UV light. I finished the work on the bridge and heard no more scary sounds. Done for the day.

"When are you going to paint this forest?" John's booming voice the next morning.

"What? It is painted," I replied. "As I told you yesterday, I just have a couple of figures left to paint."

John looked around, then turned back to me. "There's no color in here, dammit! Fix it!" He stormed off.

Stephanie had come in with John, but remained in the room when he left. She smiled at me as I said, "I don't understand. He says there's no color. What ... ?" And then it hit me. "He's color blind, isn't he?"

She grinned. "Yes, he is."

"Which means," I said, "he can't see green. To him, the forest looks like shades of grey."

"Yes."

"Why didn't you tell me before?"

"He doesn't want anyone to know."

"But that's stup...." I stopped myself. "Sorry."

Stephanie shook her head. "It's okay. Is there anything you could do so he will see more colors?"

"Yes. I can do something. But it will take a couple more days."

"That's okay. I'll tell him you're putting more color in the forest."

I set about adding different colors to the foliage and putting in more branches and vines that I could paint various colors.

"This looks great—finally!" John turned, taking in the whole room. "I like it. Now, on to the other rooms? Right?"

"Right."

He left. Stephanie had a big smile on her face, "A purple forest?"

"Hey! Whatever works," I replied.

I heard an unwanted, now familiar sound on the floor. "It" was back—and Stephanie had heard it.

"What was that?" she asked, her eyes darting around the room.

"Nothing." I took her by the arm. "Time to go." Leaving the purple forest together, I shouted, "Ed!"

Girl in bridge

CHAPTER 6
BLOOD RED HAND

I reached down to dip my artist brush into the container of red paint. The paint appeared much closer than it was. Because I was wearing 3-D glasses, I misjudged, and stuck my brush—and my hand—into the paint.

I laughed. "Damn!"

"Way to go, R.J.," said Brad, who sat beside me in the darkened room.

The UV black lights were on. I was experimenting, on a wood panel in front of me, with various colors of black-light paint and regular house paint. I removed the 3-D digital glasses and looked at my dripping hand and brush. I picked up a rag to wipe off the paint.

Brad took my 3-D glasses and put them on. "Very cool!" he said, looking down into the UV paint can. "The red paint looks like it's a foot or more above the can."

"Yeah, that's how I ended up like this," I said, holding my hand up. "You can't judge how far you should actually reach to get paint on the brush."

"That was funny," he remarked with a grin.

I stared at him. "For you."

We had five open cans of ultraviolet paint on the floor: red, blue, white, green, and yellow. Beside them were the same colors of regular house paint, along with a can of flat black. The glow of the UV colors lit us up.

Continuing my experiment, I painted swaths of UV paint, interspersed with thin lines of black paint. I put the 3-D glasses back on so that I could see which colors sank into the surface, and which appeared to come off the surface, when wearing 3-D glasses.

When I'd worked with these paints at Walt Disney World, my only purpose was to create a special lighting effect under UV light, in attractions such as the Haunted Mansion, Peter Pan's Flight, Snow White's Adventure, and Mr. Toad's Wild Ride. With the advent of these 3-D glasses, which guests would wear while touring a 3-D haunted attraction, I could create figures and sets that appeared to move, rotate, and reach out toward them. This was why I had to experiment with all this paint mixing.

"Boy, are we gonna have fun with these glasses!" I said. Looking at Brad, I could see his smiling teeth, glowing in the UV light.

I'd already been designing sets for theatres and theme parks as diverse as Dollywood and Washington & Lee University, but I wanted to branch out, because the growth in Halloween haunted houses and hayrides was exploding. Most of these venues weren't using black light yet, and I knew I could show them something new and innovative.

As a result, here we were, in the large studio I'd rented—in Virginia, where we now lived. It was later in the day, after my mixing experiments.

"So, what's next?" asked Brad.

"We need to make a figure that will pop out of a standing coffin. The guest will be startled when it jumps out at them, and then, because they're wearing 3-D glasses, and we've painted it with UV paints, it will appear much closer to them than it really is."

Brad's job was to work on the pneumatics of the figure, while I did the artwork. I would also paint some 3-D, special effects panels, and ghoulish portraits. Everything would be combined for a display booth at a large convention in Chicago, where owners of haunted attractions would be looking for new scares.

I might be afraid of things in the dark, but I've never been afraid of taking chances on something new. Even though my assistant, Brad, was skeptical about my spending money to attend this convention, I was convinced it would pay off.

I created a rotting figure, then painted it with UV paint. The inside of the coffin went from black on the sides, to a bright UV blue at the back. Once Brad had the pneumatics installed, we stood the coffin up on end, with the figure inside. All set. Black lights on. 3-D glasses on.

The coffin door opened very slowly. Nice effect. 3-D painting, good. The figure moved out of the coffin, straight at us—not quickly as we thought it would but v-e-r-r-r-y-y, very slowly. Its forward movement stopped, then it reversed back into the coffin v-e-r-r-r-y-y, very slowly.

Long pause.

"Well, that sucks!" I said as we both laughed. "Apparently, we're good at making figures and painting them, but not good at animating them."

We both just stood there, watching the slowly moving figure go in and out, in and out of the coffin. Finally, I managed to say something. "Let's just have the coffin open and close. The rotting corpse can just stay still; no movement." We laughed again as we watched our failed effort continue to move—very slowly.

My sides hurt from laughing. "Turn it off. I can't take anymore."

Brad pulled the plug, and said, "Damn the dead guy!"

CHAPTER 7
THE DOG SAW IT— ASK RASCAL!

The white light flashed once. "That's it. Don't do that again!"

"Too bright?" Brad was holding the small light in his hand. It was aimed at me.

"Perfect. We can mount that on the back wall of our convention booth. Black lights always on, and then, once a minute the timer will flash the white light."

I looked around our black-light room at the UV special-effects paintings, faces, skeletons, geometric patterns, a snake pit, a rat, a spider. These 3-D effects were perfect for the Chicago convention show a week away. I'd bought a used box truck to haul everything in, and we had brochures and business cards ready.

That evening, I sat in our den at home with Suzanne, relaxing with a drink. We'd both always wanted to move out of Florida, to enjoy the four seasons. (I am originally from St. Charles, Illinois, and Suzanne is from St. Louis.) About five years earlier, we had moved to a small town in the Shenandoah Valley of Virginia. I now had my own scenic design studio there, and we had recently bought a beautiful, two-story home, that had been built in 1885.

We talked about the upcoming trip to Chicago, during commercial breaks of *X-Files*.

"I got the confirmation for your hotel rooms," Suzanne said.

"Great. Three nights, right?"

"Right." She gave me a half smile. "I'm going to miss you." Over the years, we've worked together on theatre projects, special events, parades, half-time shows, scripts for TV, and our Walt Disney World careers—the list goes on. This time, however, we decided that Brad and I could handle the convention show booth, and Suzanne could stay home to take care of the dogs, and continue decorating our new home.

When another commercial came on, I got up from the couch. "Time for some M & M's." The crystal bowl that contained my favorite candy snack was two rooms away, on the coffee table in the living room. This kept me from constantly consuming my favorite thing—chocolate—because I had to "travel" to get any. I'd spent several months reducing my weight by sixty pounds (which I've managed to maintain all the years since—very proud of that), and having the candy out of easy reach helped in that effort.

I passed through Suzanne's study, and into the living room. One small lamp was lit in there. As usual, our large, Karelian Bear Dog, Rascal, was right by my side. As I took my handful of candy, I noticed he was looking out toward the foyer and the front door.

"Whatcha doin,' Rascal?" He stood there, not moving a muscle. Rascal's breed was originally raised to hunt bear in Finland, where they originated. They were brought to the U.S. to chase grizzly bears out of populated areas in the West. Although great with kids, and very loving, I trusted Rascal to protect me.

"Rascal?" He didn't move, but emitted a low growl. The hair stood up on my neck. I stared at the opening into the foyer, trying to observe some kind of movement in the hall. Nothing.

I moved slowly toward the door, telling Rascal to stay with me. He did just that, his side touching my leg. I looked toward the front door. No one out there. Rascal growled again. I jumped, and looked down at him. He was now facing the stairway that went up to the second floor. My eyes followed where he was looking.

A blue-and-white shimmering light, about eighteen inches wide and four to five feet tall, was floating in the air, halfway up the stairs. I managed to squeal out, "Rascal." He quickly walked up the stairs, tail wagging, to the ghostly image moving down toward him, stopping when they met. His tail was still wagging as the shimmering light faded, and then disappeared. Rascal remained on the step, momentarily, sniffing around, then came back down to my side. He looked like he was smiling. Yes, I think dogs can smile!

"Okay, boy? Uh-huh. Let's go back to the den, shall we?" Rascal, tail still wagging, padded beside me into the den.

Suzanne looked at me. Her brow furrowed. "Are you all right? You look like you've seen a ghost."

"Um, yeah." I sat down. Rascal jumped up on the couch and laid down between us.

"What?" Suzanne asked, as I tried to relax my frowning face.

"I—uh—I think I did see a ghost."

Suzanne laughed. "Sure you did!"

"No, seriously. I ... we ... saw a ghost, on the stairs. Ask Rascal."

Rascal raised his head, and thumped his tail on the couch.

I related what we'd just experienced in the foyer. She went with me and Rascal to investigate. We turned on all the lights in the hallway and the staircase. Suzanne looked up the stairs and around the foyer, then at me and Rascal, and shook her head.

"You are kidding me, right?"

"Ask Rascal. He saw it first!"

In the five years we lived in that house, before moving to Chicago, we would be visited by that ghost many times. Suzanne became a believer after seeing the image upstairs, and others in our family saw her as well over the years.

Suzanne researched the history of the house and discovered that the family who originally lived there for nearly fifty years had a daughter, Lucy, an artist, who had died in the house. Lucy began to materialize in more recognizable form, and we could tell, from her dress, that she came from the late 1800s. We have a picture of her and her family, seated on the steps of that house, taken around 1901.

"Lucy" did funny things, like moving chairs in the dining room to spots near the large windows, and she would unscrew light bulbs in the fixtures throughout the house (guess she wanted things to be as they were when she lived there; no electricity). We would sometimes, in the night, hear doors opening and closing, or soft sounds, but she was never scary, and we actually enjoyed having a resident ghost.

When I told Brad the story about Rascal and discovering Lucy, he kidded me, and said I imagined her. My answer to him was, "The dog saw her. Ask Rascal!" This would be a recurring conversation as he and I travelled to Chicago for the convention.

Our historic, and haunted, house

Our hall stairway, where the ghost first appeared

Rascal, the dog who saw a ghost

CHAPTER 8
SELLING MYSELF IN CHICAGO

"I was a Disney artist," I would say, as people came by, or near, our eight-foot booth, which was stuck in a corner. It was our first day of the convention. This was a huge venue, but the area for dark rides, scares, Halloween merchandise, and haunted house things was in a relatively small section of the gigantic hall. Halloween was a new and growing market, and it was about to escalate across the United States.

Some of the animatronic figures were impressive. One booth had a rotting skeleton in a bed that would suddenly fly up and out, right at the viewers. Everyone jumped and screamed, then laughed whenever that happened. *I should hire them to fix our coffin skeleton*, I thought. Oh, well.

I was selling my artistic abilities like never before. I told Brad if he had a customer, to make sure he kept him or her interested until I could talk to them. These people came from all over the U.S., to Chicago, to view new products, new scares; any new ideas for their haunted houses. Their attractions ranged from small mom-and-pop ventures in a garage, to theme parks such as Six Flags. There was a lot for them to see, but, because we were tucked away in a corner, we needed to entice them to come over to our booth.

"Brad, I don't think we're going anywhere with the guy in the coffin. Turn him off and leave the lid open. I think our best bet is to sell my ability to create really good 3-D effects in black light, with the other examples we have here." I was passionate. "We've got to get them over here and get the 3-D glasses on them." Brad nodded.

"Once we do that, it will be easier to talk to them about hiring me to paint 3-D effects in their attractions."

"I agree," said Brad, nodding again.

I made a quick sign that read, "3-D Black-Light Painting by Former Disney Artist." It helped some. Brad went into the crowd with brochures and business cards. That helped, too. By late afternoon of that first day, we had begun to get some interested people.

That night, in a bar near our hotel, we were a little depressed, but not defeated.

The second day, I was talking to Becky Bartling, a lovely woman from the Del Mar Racetrack in southern California. She told me about the Halloween attraction they wanted to create there, in two large barns. Brad stood nearby, talking to another potential client. He excused himself as he passed me a note. I continued talking to Becky, who was wearing a pair of our 3-D glasses, and who seemed quite interested in my pitch.

I discreetly opened the note, which read, "How much for painting?—an amount per day." I quickly wrote a figure, making sure no one near me could see what I was writing. I handed it back to Brad, who read it and blurted loudly, "What?!"

Becky stopped talking in mid-sentence. She and I looked at Brad in surprise, as did the man he'd been talking to.

"You okay, Brad?" I gave him a concerned smile.

"Yeah ... yes. Sorry."

He returned to his potential client and showed him the paper. The man turned and walked away. I continued talking to Becky as if nothing had happened. After more discussion, she asked how much my fee was. Without batting an eye, I replied, "$500.00 a day," then quickly added, "I can paint very fast, and give you quality results."

Selling Myself in Chicago 49

She thought for a moment. "How long would it take you to paint four, good-sized rooms, with trees in one and the Devil in Hell in the other three?"

After a moment's thought, I gave her an answer. I saw Brad, out of the corner of my eye, staring at me like I was nuts.

"Well, thank you," said Becky. "I'll get back to you." She handed me the 3-D glasses and walked away. The crowds were thinning out by now.

"Five hundred dollars a day?!" Brad was incredulous.

"Sure." I looked at my watch. It was almost five o-clock. "Let's close up and get dinner and a drink. I think tomorrow will be busier." Pause. "I hope."

"I think we could use more than one drink," Brad replied, as he began closing down our booth.

Brad and I originally expected to sell figures I'd paint which we could manufacture in my Virginia studio and then ship to clients. We were now playing this convention by ear, and on the run. Clients had begun asking us if I would travel to their attractions and paint entire rooms. Since we hadn't expected this, we had no set fee for services, and I was winging it.

Over dinner and drinks, we talked about the $500-per-day fee. Brad thought it was too high. I insisted we stay with that amount, and once we got one contract, I could show how much I could do in one day's work. I had to believe in myself.

The next day of the show, it was busier. I was keeping my fingers crossed. We met more clients, and quoted our daily fee. Some walked off, shaking their heads, but some stayed and discussed possibilities.

One man asked all kinds of questions, but initially, didn't tell us what his attraction was, or its location. He and his business partner did seem quite interested, though. I was just hoping I hadn't screwed up a good opportunity. After a few more minutes, we learned that his name was

Jim Feltes, and he and his family owned Sonny Acres Farm in West Chicago. He explained that every September and October, they staged a huge Halloween experience featuring haunted barns, carnival rides, a petting zoo, food, merchandise, and a big haunted hayride.

After more discussion with him, he said he wanted me to paint black-light figures in the barns, and create some new figures for the hayride. I said that Suzanne would accompany me to help out. He agreed to a three-day contract, and said that Suzanne and I could stay in his mother's historic farmhouse.

Once we completed arrangements with him, and he left, Brad said, "Wow!"

"Yeah, we're on the right track. I feel it."

And then Becky Bartling came back. She wanted me to come to Del Mar for five days. I explained to her that my wife would be coming with me as my assistant (it was a great way for us to be together).

I told Brad that he would remain in Virginia to run the studio in my absence. "Terrific! I can do that."

We weren't finished yet, either. Eric Prevratil, from the HMS *Queen Mary* (one of the most regal ocean liners, now permanently docked in Long Beach as a hotel and convention venue), came back to our booth. He signed a ten-day contract, which included a stateroom on the *Queen Mary* for Suzanne and me while we worked there!

This would be the only time we participated in this Chicago show. But it had resulted in the explosion of the Halloween business—for us!

CHAPTER 9
SONNY ACRES

"I remember this farm."

Suzanne and I were standing beside our new car, looking at the farmhouse, barn, and other buildings.

"We would drive past here when I was little. We'd drive on North Avenue, which was just two lanes then, from St. Charles to Chicago. Thirty miles. That was a long drive on two lanes in the late 1940s."

Suzanne looked at the now historic two-story farmhouse and the big red barn, both in beautiful condition.

"Really?"

"Yeah. This was all farm land out here, for miles." I gestured with my hand, remembering my three favorite things about my first trip to Chicago at the age of five: 1) seeing this farm as we drove by; 2) stopping at Kiddieland where I rode a pony in circles; and 3) watching the Buckingham Fountain in Grant Park downtown.

We walked into the produce stand at the front of the property and asked for Jim Feltes. A few minutes later, he was giving us a tour of his farm and introducing us to some of his siblings. He had seven brothers and one sister.

He explained that his mother and father had owned the farm "forever," and had opened a roadside stand in 1951, which became an instant success. His mother still lived in the farmhouse, built in 1895. She had inherited the farm from her parents, and her grandparents, the Nagels, were German immigrants and the original owners of the homestead. In recent years, he and his siblings had sold some of the land, part of which was now a housing development, but some was still kept for farming. Jim had begun the haunted house and hayride attractions.

He took us to the farmhouse and introduced us to his charming mother, Ramona. We were immediately taken with the house. It reminded me of my Swedish grandparents' house, which is still standing in St. Charles, Illinois, just five miles west of where we were standing in this historic home. Ramona showed us to our bedroom on the second floor, and as we were unpacking, we were intrigued by the unusual bedside lamp, which we learned from Ramona had been made from a five-inch diameter shell from a deck gun. Her husband had brought it back from his navy engagement in WWII. It had beautiful etchings on it.

Half an hour later, I was in black light again ... in a barn. Wood, hay, spider webs ... *hey, wait a minute! One of my least favorite things: spiders. Great! Well, just have to be careful. Not poisonous ... mostly. Not big ... Oh, look, a Daddy Long Legs! Not dangerous and actually pretty cool.* Lots of thoughts to myself as I made my way down the passages to the first figures that had been created. Suzanne was not with me, as most of the painting on this job would be done by me. She had gone into downtown Chicago to spend time with our son, Sean. He'd graduated from Florida State University, then moved to Chicago to pursue his acting career.

I would quickly discover how well walk-through haunted houses worked, if you kept the guests confined to a maze of narrow passageways and small rooms. This was much different from Disney's Haunted Mansion where guests rode in a confined car, and the rooms were much bigger. When you have the guests walking in big rooms, they will spread out and miss the scares, or see the scares coming—which defeats the scares.

The figures in the Sonny Acres barn, which had been painted with inexpensive fluorescent paint, didn't work very well. I would see this in other haunts in the years to come. To be truly effective, high-powered, latex ultraviolet paint has to be used. This paint is so intense that, when you open the can lid, in UV lighting the color—red, yellow, blue, whatever—will bathe you in that color.

At Walt Disney World, we used Shannon Glow brand, which came in a wide range of colors, though Shannon seemed to be a small operation. Wildfire brand was becoming the brand to use. I had five gallons of Wildfire paint for this job: red, yellow, blue, green, and white. I had those same colors in flat latex house paints, to mix with the UV paints for shading. I also had flat latex black; very important.

None of the work I would do at Sonny Acres required 3-D glasses. This was straight-on, normal black-light painting. Not as complicated, and the same techniques I had used at Walt Disney World when painting attraction figures.

I made mental notes of the best scares as I worked my way through the barn. I repainted faces, figures, hands, and even signs, some made to look as though they were dripping blood. Suddenly, something brushed the back of my head. I jumped, and almost kicked over some paint. I turned around, but saw nothing. It had felt like a bug—and then I saw what it was: a long piece of straw sticking out of a hay bale! I checked around to make sure I was alone. *Okay. Deep breath. You're safe.*

Next day, I finished in the big barn, and Jim gave me a ride in his golf cart through the haunted hayride. He would stop to explain different scares and show me where he wanted me to paint some things in black light. I'd have to come back at night to do those. Three of my favorite scares he'd created involved real actors, one in black light.

The first was a guy who would repel fast, down a large tree, right above the hay wagon full of guests. He was fully costumed as the alien in the film *Predator*, and he glowed in the UV light. Another was a stuntman who set himself on fire.

"Jim."

"Yes?"

"How many times a night does he do that?"

"A lot. But he only sets part of himself on fire."

"He's nuts!"

"Yes!"

Don't ever try that stunt! I thought about our good friend, Tony Cecere, a stuntman considered one of the greatest in Hollywood, known for his fire stunts in such movies as *Swamp Thing*, *Terminator 2*, *Ghostbusters* (Tony was the Sta-Puff Marshmallow Man), and most of Wes Craven's films. Tony was incredible and highly trained. I hoped this guy on the hayride was, too.

Another great scare came when the hayride passed by the swamp bog and corn field. A ghoul would rise up out of the darkened bog to surprise and terrify the guests. Creepy!

Jim also pointed out a huge oak tree, at a bend in the trail. "Right there, I want a big scare next year. Can you come up with something?"

"Sure." *I'll be back here next year; good!*

During the three days we stayed at the Sonny Acres farmhouse, we had a wonderful time with Jim's mother. Not only was she a great cook, but she told us all about the history of the farm and the house. When she learned that I had served in Vietnam, and was a military history buff, she shared the story about her husband's time during WWII. She explained that the etchings on the lamp in our room were done by him. They depicted battles he was in.

"He was a naval officer aboard the USS *Oklahoma*," she said.

"Was he aboard on December 7, when the Japanese attacked Pearl Harbor?"

"No. He got out of the navy one month before Pearl Harbor." There was silence for a moment.

I finally said, in a quiet tone, "He lost friends on that ship."

"A lot of friends," she answered. "He re-enlisted immediately and served aboard another ship during the war."

"Wow," was all I could say.

"I have the two diaries he wrote during the War. Would you like to read them?"

"Absolutely."

Suzanne and I were up until after 2 a.m. the next morning, reading the two pocket-sized, worn leather diaries. They contained stunning accounts of battles at sea, some with minute-to-minute entries, jotted down by her husband while he was on the bridge of his ship, during kamikaze attacks.

The following year, Suzanne stayed home as Brad and I went back to Sonny Acres Farm to install some new figures in the not-so-scary children's haunted barn. We also installed the huge monster with the giant claws. Yes, the very same monster in chapter one ... where I had the run-in with the scary black cat.

My son, Sean, and his two roommates, Steve and Arik, were hired by Jim to perform scares in the haunted hayride. (They had so much fun, they did it for a second year.) Steve came up with the idea of laying in the cornfield bog and rising up out of it, just as the hay wagon rolled by. Steve would jump up on the side of the wagon, and reach for the guests, who would scream and lean away from him, only to have Sean and Arik suddenly appear on the other side of the wagon. Screams galore!

Sonny Acres is still going strong today—and some of my work is still there, including the huge monster on the hayride. Jim added a bubble machine and strobe light to that figure, which enhances the scare in black light.

Now that we live in the Chicago area, our whole family was treated to a private hayride by Jim, when we all were there last Halloween.

I wonder if that damn black cat is still there. I know; he would be a very old, black cat. BUT! It's a cat!

CHAPTER 10
SCREAM ZONE

A rat hissed at the young woman in front of me. She screamed and backed up—into me. I could see the rat's head with its beady, red eyes, peering through a black hole in the wall.

"Sorry," the girl said sheepishly. She moved past the rat. I followed. The rat's eyes followed me as I went past, and its sharp teeth glowed in the black light. I caught up to the girl and four other people, all wearing 3-D glasses (as was I). They were walking slowly, and I actually bumped into them as we entered a pitch dark area.

I began to be aware of something, over the heads of those in front of me. It was a chain link fence, eight feet high. The setting behind the fence was one of an alley littered with metal garbage cans, some with lids on, and garbage strewn across the narrow passage. Blood! Blood was everywhere: on a brick wall, on the concrete floor, on the chain link, and on a blanket covering a man. There was fear in his eyes as he looked up, and to our right, toward the dark alley beyond us. Someone in our group said, "Yuck!" and another person laughed, nervously.

Suddenly, a screaming man ran out of the dark alley, kicking trash cans and lids across the area. The noise was deafening! He jumped on the chain link fence and screamed at us, his teeth bared. His skin was gray, and pieces of flesh hung from his rotting face. Everyone jumped in terror and screamed bloody murder!

Screams turned to laughter as everyone ran past other buildings, into the darkness. I stopped to look into the eyes of the zombie still clinging to the chain link. He stopped screaming. He smiled.

"How was that?"

I started laughing. "Perfect. Absolutely perfect."

We could hear a dog growl, then bark, and a loud crash. These sounds were followed by more screams and laughter.

"Ah, they just found the dog!" Just then, two of the people I'd been following appeared out of the darkness. "You're going the wrong way," I told them. "Turn around."

"You mean we have to go back past that dog again?"

"Yes, you do. Have fun!"

As they disappeared, the "zombie actor" and I laughed at them.

"This may be the best scare ever. I'd better get going. There's another group coming behind me," I told him.

As the actor went back into the dark alley to await the next "visitors," he said to me, "I'm having a blast!"

The "Scream Zone" at Del Mar Racetrack, near San Diego, California, was a few days from opening. We were doing a dry run, with some Del Mar employees as our "guinea pigs," to test how well our scares would work on paying customers.

This was the third year in a row that Suzanne and I had come to Del Mar to design, supervise construction and rigging, and paint this 3-D haunted house. The layout was in two huge, side by side barns on the racetrack grounds, mere yards from the first turn of the racetrack itself. As we worked each afternoon, we could hear—and feel the vibration of—the running horses. If we looked out the open barn doors, we could see the magnificent creatures as they galloped past. We never tired of those moments.

It was early August 2002, and it would be mid-September before we finished. The first year (2000) that we did the Scream Zone, it only took five days because we only did 3-D painting in four rooms. The next year, we came back and created a whole new, 3-D haunted attraction. It took us a month to complete it.

That was 2001. Friends of ours, Ray Scholl and Amy Reynolds, who lived nearby, offered us a bedroom in their home, which was much better than a boring hotel room—and saved us money besides. On September 11, we woke to the horrible news of an attack on our nation by terrorists. Ray, a Marine flight navigator, was in Japan with his F-18 squadron, so our first hours were spent with Amy, as we attempted to comfort her, and each other. Our daughter, Dawn, called from Virginia, and her first words to me were chilling: "Daddy, I'm so scared!" I stifled my tears and talked to her, eventually calming her somewhat. I then phoned our son, Sean, who now lived in Hollywood with his girlfriend, Sande. They were shaken, but talking to them helped all of us.

We were supposed to work that day, and did go to the racetrack, but it was impossible to focus on what now seemed unimportant tasks. By noon, the Del Mar front office announced that those who were there working should come to the racetrack lounge. We were provided with a buffet lunch, as we continued to watch TV screens. After that, everyone was sent home. For every American, 9/11/2001 evokes specific memories.

By the third year, 2002, we had three employees hired just for the construction of the haunted house. One of them, Steve Burr, was a former Marine, proficient at everything from building to mechanical and electrical work. He had worked with us all three years, and I put him in charge of the other two assistants. We had our own office for the first time that year, which helped Suzanne coordinate the work and gave me a space where I could lay out my floor plan designs as well as my sketches of ideas for the attraction.

We were happy that our work meant we were in San

Diego for Amy and Ray's wedding. Even better, they let us stay at their home while they went on their honeymoon. To add to that fun, we got to dog-sit their canine, Toby—who happily greeted us each evening.

The Del Mar Scream Zone had different themed areas and rooms each year. That gave me the opportunity to experiment in 3-D painting and scares. Becky Bartling gave me full rein to explore lots of new ideas. One of those was the Silent Hill area I just described. It had been six weeks of work this time, and we were nearly finished. We were now working on two of my favorite designs: Chucky's Room and The Mummy Room.

The first step for me, in these rooms, was to lay out areas or shapes that Suzanne would paint with white latex. I would then paint over the white, with black-light and latex paint, creating the images in 3-D. She'd already done the Mummy Room and had started on Chucky's Room, while I worked on my mummies. We had a roll-around table on which we had drinks, snacks, and our CD player, and we would place it midway between our work spaces.

Suzanne would change out the CDs, most of which had been created by our son, Sean, for our personal use. They had music selections from the 1930s to the present day, interspersed with audio clips from movies and TV shows. They could be heard throughout the barns. All the workers loved them, and would try to be the first to guess what show or movie a clip was from.

"My name is Inigo Montoya. You killed my father; prepare to die!"

Princess Bride, someone would yell from another room.

When I took Suzanne into Chucky's Room to show her what to paint, she looked around and said, "This is a lot of circles."

"Yeah," I said, "a lot of doll's heads."

"Definitely weird."

"Yes." I left her and returned to my mummies.

The entire room was painted to look like the inside of an Egyptian tomb. Hieroglyphics filled two six-inch-high bands that circled the room, at the top of the walls. I hid Suzanne's name, and mine, in the hieroglyphics. The symbols looked authentic, but I had no idea what I was writing!

Steve came in while I was working and looked at the Egyptian writings. "Do you know what all this says?"

"Not a clue."

He laughed. "Looks good, anyway. Hope it doesn't say something bad."

"Right," I answered. "But I'm not too worried about hieroglyphic scholars coming through here."

"True."

I was just finishing the red eyes of the last mummy when Becky Bartling joined us.

"This looks great," she said.

I handed her a pair of 3-D glasses. "Go back in the dark hallway, put these on, and then walk back." When she was out of the room, I instructed Steve to go behind the wall and "set up the scare."

In this tomb scene, there were six two-foot by six-foot, four-inch alcoves, three on each side of the room. Each alcove appeared to be set in sandstone block. Inside each alcove were skeleton soldiers, wearing decorative waistcloths, sandals, and bejeweled head gear. Each held a sword, and each was in a different, menacing pose. With the 3-D glasses on, the alcoves looked two feet deep, and the figures seemed to rotate and turn toward you, as you moved through the room. One skeleton's head lay at its feet, and a yellow-and-red snake curled around its rib cage. The snake's head, mouth open, looked ready to strike, and he followed you as you walked past.

Becky reappeared, smiling as she looked around. When she approached the third skeleton to her right, its screaming face seeming to be eighteen inches off the wall, she put her hand into the 3-D illusion, saying, "This is great, but what is the surprise scare?" A hidden door, on which the skeleton was painted, suddenly opened inward, Steve screamed at her, then slammed the door.

"Shit!" Becky screamed, then laughed. "That's ... really ... good."

Steve opened the hidden door again, a smile on his face. "The actor who will hide back here will wear a costume, similar to the figure's. A drop lock on the back of the door will protect him or her, for safety's sake."

"I like it." All three of us went to the next room, where Suzanne was busy painting white circles. "What's this room going to be?" Becky asked.

"Floating doll's heads, nasty ones. A weird carpet will be painted on the floor, that will appear to be floating; all because of the 3-D glasses. But when they step "up" on it, their foot will look like its sinking, through the carpet, and into nothingness."

"What goes in this corner?" She pointed at a shelf about five feet off the floor.

"Chucky. With a bloody knife," I said, grinning. "And, while guests are enjoying the 3-D, and then Chucky, a bassinet under Chucky will start rocking, and a bloody baby doll will rise out of it."

"Creepy!"

"That's when an actor, in bloody clothes, will come through the hidden door, in the wall behind the guests."

"So, just one actor each in this room and the Egyptian room?"

"Yes, the actors will be able to keep the guests moving forward through the house, as they run away from these scares," I explained.

"Everything is looking great, R.J.," Becky said. "Have you and Suzanne had any free time to go over and see one of the races?"

"We're planning to, now that we're nearly done here."

After lunch one day, we changed into "nice clothes" and

made our way toward the racetrack. To get to the main entrance, we walked between the stables. Grooms readied horses for races, and jockeys, in their silks, passed by us. We had to brush dust off our shoes before entering the main building.

The Spanish architecture of Del Mar Racetrack was unique. Built in 1937 by Bing Crosby, and his friends, including Pat O'Brien, Gary Cooper, Joe E. Brown, Oliver Hardy, and Charles S. Howard (owner of champion racehorse Seabiscuit), it is the second largest racing venue in the United States. Bing Crosby personally greeted the first visitors on opening day. It was closed during WWII, used for training Marines, and later as a manufacturing site for B-17 bomber parts.

Suzanne and I had special badges clipped to our shirts that allowed us entry into all the areas of the racetrack. We went to the paddock to view the horses getting ready to race, then up to make a bet before going into the viewing stands. We won $98.00 on a $4.00 bet! Pure luck because we had no idea what we were doing. We just liked the name of the horse we bet on.

Death in the alley of Silent Hill

Silent Hill scene in Scream Zone

Del Mar Racetrack clubhouse

Del Mar Racetrack, first turn

Horse exercise area at Del Mar Racetrack

Mummy tomb in Scream Zone

Painting in Scream Zone mummy room

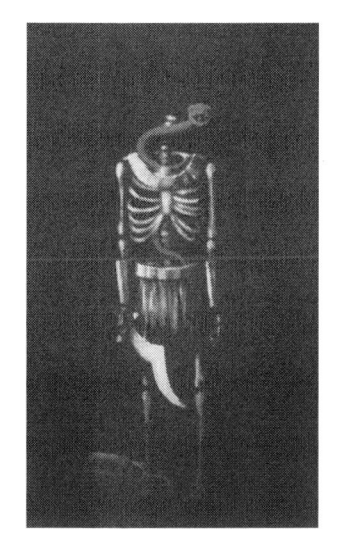

Mummy soldiers in Scream Zone

Mummy in Scream Zone

CHAPTER 11
INTO THE JAWS OF A CLOWN

A horse whinnied. I looked at Steve. "That sounds like a horse is in our barn."

"Sure does."

I stopped painting. He stopped working on the rigging of lights. We walked farther into the haunted maze and looked around.

"No horse." It whinnied again.

"You first," Steve said, pointing to the next room. We did a total walk-through of the attraction, meeting Suzanne at the exit.

"What are you two up to?" she asked.

"We're looking for a horse."

"What?"

"We're loo…. Sorry. That sounds stupid. We're surrounded by horses here."

"Ya' think?" she answered, sarcasm in her tone.

Steve and I explained the sounds we'd heard, which seemed to come from inside the house.

"I didn't hear anything in here," she said.

We decided to stop looking. Never heard the horse "in" the house or barn again.

Ghost horse?

Steve and I headed back to work, in the first room of the haunted house, a cave with surprises. This area was where the guests were greeted by an actor who had them put on their 3-D glasses, then instructed them to find their way out of the cave while stretching their arms out in front of them. They soon learned why they had to walk that way. The room appeared to have three exits, but only one was real; the others were painted on a flat wall to resemble the real exit.

On the walls, I painted red and blue trailing vines that continued onto the floor and became a swirling mass around a bottomless pit (in actuality, it was just a big, black circle painted onto the floor). It was fun to watch the guests make a big deal of avoiding this black hole by stepping carefully around it.

When designing an eclectic haunted house, it's important to include a variety of scares, from funny to creepy to outright frightening. I've always tried to avoid gory and bloody, but, since the owners were the deciding force, I sometimes had to abide by their concepts.

My Walt Disney World experience and training always influence the physical layout of an attraction. Disney's mantra of "Safety, Courtesy, Capacity, Show" is constantly in my mind. Emergency exits, safety of both guests and employees, guest flow, actor placement and movement, backstage access for technicians, and the lighting and sound issues are all part of my detailed drawings.

I've been a guest in some haunted houses that scared me to death: not from the haunts, but from the appalling lack of safety concerns—elements such as not enough emergency exits, or poorly marked ones, inadequate, jerry-rigged or just plain "bad" electrical connections, poor construction including flammable materials, and objects that can impede guest flow or cause guests to trip or be injured. I do know of one haunted house that burned to the ground; luckily in the middle of the night, and no one was harmed!

Design of these disasters, created only to make money for a month, are usually amateurish, and there really is no "design;" the houses are just one room after another with no planned show, transitions, or flow. In addition, they do not employ enough people, including good actors, to enhance the guest experience.

You can't just have a body, in a costume, standing in the middle of a room doing nothing, and call that "an actor." I've even been aware of instances where the talent was voluntary (no pay involved), and the employees would work one night, never to be seen again. I always try to make a first-time owner of a haunted attraction understand the reason he must pay the talent. Standing in the same room, night after night, and doing the same scare to hundreds of people, gets old fast. Volunteers are the first to quit this type of job.

Over the years, I am happy to say, I have seen regulations by cities and states become much stricter regarding safety issues in these temporary attractions. In Illinois, for example, all haunted houses are required to have a working sprinkler system.

The Del Mar Scream Zone was the perfect example of a haunted attraction that adhered to all of the concerns I just outlined. It was the main reason why I was always happy to return there each year.

I was standing in the cemetery room. (We're now back at the Scream Zone, my third year there.) I was happy about how well the transition and flow worked for this room, and those beyond. I stepped out of the mausoleum. Tombstones … a lot of tombstones stretched out before me up a hill, and into the distance. A small grey something flew past my feet. "Dammit!" I yelled, as my heart skipped a beat. It ran around the mausoleum, and disappeared. I recognized the barn cat, and yelled, "Stop doing that!"

"Are you okay?" Suzanne said, entering the cemetery.

"I'm fine. The cat scared me."

"Again?"

"Yes. It's bad enough it surprises me by running full speed past me. I'm also terrified of what it's chasing, or worse, what it's running from!" I walked over to where the cat had disappeared, and peeked around the corner. Totally dark. Couldn't see anything. I turned on my flashlight and almost jumped out of my shoes, as two yellow eyes stared back at me.

"Damn you!" The cat took off. I chuckled and walked back to Suzanne.

"What now?" She asked.

"I think that nasty feline is messing with me."

I walked back over to the mausoleum I'd been painting, and turned to Suzanne.

"Step inside that dark alcove. I want to see if the lighting is right." She stepped into the open doorway and was enveloped in darkness. "Perfect! You can come out. What a great hiding place for an actor!"

When guests entered the cemetery room, they were facing the rear of the first mausoleum. They would walk around it to enter the main part of the cemetery, their attention focused on a hill where hundreds of tombstones stood. A three-foot-high wall guided their path through the cemetery. A second mausoleum was on their right, and the third was directly in front of them. Steve had built the mausoleums, each about five-feet square and eight-feet high; all of different designs.

The guests would be looking at the second and third mausoleums, expecting an actor to pop out of one. These were decoys. With their attention diverted, an actor came out, behind them, from the first mausoleum to scare them. I would have liked a pop-up head, like the ones I had painted for WDW's Haunted Mansion, to appear from behind a tombstone, but that never happened.

Leaving the cemetery, the guests entered a completely dark passage—a transition I designed on purpose. Their movements would activate a small strobe light, aimed at an actor who was hiding in the darkness. This did two things: 1) it was a great scare, and 2) it really messed with the guests' eyes!

Into the Jaws of a Clown 73

Beyond this dark hallway was the next-to-the-last room: the toxic waste room. Real metal drums were used, and I created red and green toxic fluids, oozing out of them and onto the floor. Other 3-D effects included bodies and body parts, floating in the waste. My favorite creation was the image of a head I painted, which rose up out of the waste that swirled around the guests' feet and legs. Steve took a huge tube (from the inside of a carpet roll), and fashioned it into a three-feet-wide by eight-feet-high half-circle "drum," and hinged it to a wall as a hiding place for an actor. I painted this prop to look like a stack of real toxic waste drums, oozing liquid. One of the benefits, in black light 3-D, was the ability to make a small (unseen by the guests) peephole for an actor to look through, and know when to jump out and scare guests.

After the toxic waste room, the guests had to navigate one last dark maze. The tension was heightened for them by the sounds of a chain saw and the screams of other guests.

Almost all haunted houses wanted chain saws. Scary? Yes.

And clowns. What?

I am amazed at how many people are afraid of clowns. What happened? When did clowns cross over from the funny, goofy guys at circuses, or beloved images of childhood, to terrifying killers spreading mayhem?

It has to be horror movies. I must admit, the clown doll in the original *Poltergeist* movie was pretty damn scary!

I decided to make the finale of the Scream Zone about chain saws AND clowns. I first painted nasty looking clowns, a lot of balloons, confetti, and streamers on both the walls and the floor. No guest could escape them, and then a costumed clown with a chain saw (no blade for safety's sake, but still noisy) ran at them. Screaming and searching for the exit, the guest would suddenly realize that there was only one way out: through the mouth of a GIANT clown head, 12' feet high by 10' feet wide, painted around the barn exit door, his bottom lip and his chin painted on the floor. Beyond the door, all a guest could see was total darkness.

The ensuing mayhem was fun to watch: the chainsaw clown chasing guests, who were too frightened to go through the exit, and into the jaws of the clown! The entire time they'd be screaming and/or laughing because they wanted out.

I like all the areas of a haunted house or hayride to be good, but it's most important to capture your audience immediately as they enter, give them another great scare in the middle, and then a whiz-bang ending.

By opening with the Egyptian room and mummies, then having the middle contain Silent Hill and the Growling Dog—oh, yes, didn't tell you about the growling dog!

Remember our test group running from the zombie into darkness, and then the sound of a growling dog and other noises? Well, those guests went through an area of winding alleys surrounded by buildings and chain link fence. Moving forward, the growling dog sound grew louder. On their left side, they came upon an eight-foot high chain link fence, separating them from a blood-spattered alley with more trash cans and a dead body. Expecting another zombie, the growls of the dog came from their right side, behind more chain link.

A half-rotted, full-sized, 3-D dog figure suddenly crashed into the fence. The result of my painting, combined with the guests' view through 3-D glasses, caused the head of the dog to appear to crash through the fence at them. More screams, they run, then another zombie kicks more cans on their left.

So, great middle with zombies and creepy dog.

Then, the ending of the house—scary clown and scary chain saws. Scream Zone had it all for the guests (plus a scary cat and a ghost horse for me).

Clown Mouth

Cemetery in Scream Zone

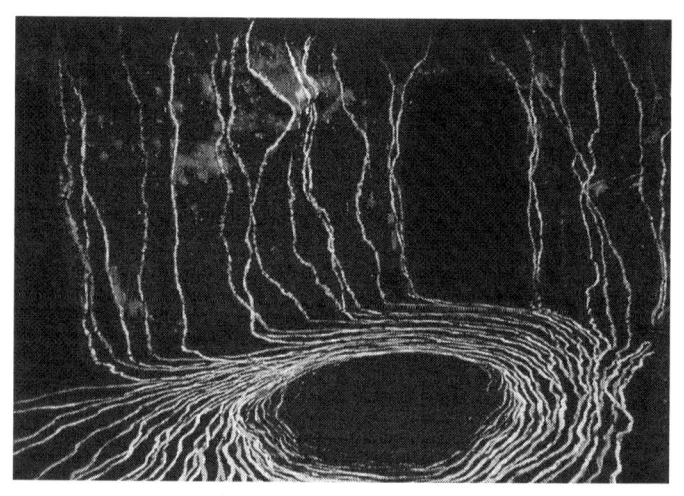

Scream Zone entrance pit

Scream Zone spectre

CHAPTER 12
WE REALLY ARE IN HELL!

It came at me. Evil, dark ... nasty. I moved away, into the sunlight, hoping the hot sun would keep it away. Perspiration dripped from my brow. It was very hot. I was miserable, and now I was being stalked by one ... no, two ... *oh crap! Back up! Back up!*

These things were ugly, and very menacing. I waved my paint rag back and forth, hoping it would keep them off me ... these damn, scary, crappy....

"Oh, damn you, get away from me!"

I must have looked silly, moving backward and swatting the air. The herd was growing. Mosquitoes! I was under attack by a herd of mosq ... *wait. A herd?*

A swarm. That's it. I laughed and swore as I retreated toward my paint and supplies, in a shady spot ten feet away. I reached into my bag and pulled out the bug spray. Time for new protection against these evil creatures.

I was not happy working on this hayride west of Boston and ... *why is it so damn hot?* I was in hell, but I was almost done with this job.

It was great to travel each year to haunted attractions around the country, painting and creating effects, and installing figures we had created back at my studio. Flying banshees, pop-up ghouls, ghosts, and yes, spiders, snakes, and rats. Really big spiders, snakes, and rats.

My work took me all over the U.S.; to Six Flags attractions in New Jersey and St. Louis, to Del Mar near San

Diego, as well as to haunted houses and hayrides in Chicago, Lockport, and Rockford, Illinois; also Warren and Niles, Michigan; Minneapolis, Minnesota; Lincoln, Nebraska; and Moorpark, California. At several locations, Suzanne & I were invited to stay in the owner's homes; other times we were in hotels.

Here, in Boston, I was repainting most of the existing structures for this hayride, which had existed for several years before I was contracted. Some building facades depicted a Western town, and were in need of refreshing, for sure. I had been asked to create a version of the man-eating plant from *Little Shop of Horrors* which, when the hay wagon would pass by, the plant would fly out the window of a shop and its mouth would open. It was odd, to me, to have this plant as part of a Western theme.

There were two technical problems with the plant. First, the owner didn't install any sound effects. Second, the guests riding on the far side of the wagon didn't experience the scare. I had suggested that the plant be put in a location where it would come down toward the wagon, to scare the occupants. My suggestion was ignored. This was one of the few haunted attraction jobs that was disappointing for me.

I finally finished painting the buildings and some signs that had been requested by the owner, and then, with amazingly few mosquito bites, I packed up my supplies and drove back to the "one-star motel" that the owner had booked for us. Suzanne had spent two days in it, with nothing to do but watch daytime TV. There was really nothing for her to help me with on the job, and I didn't want her to suffer the heat and the bugs at the work location. I was just thankful she was here to keep me sane.

Now that I was done, we could look forward to spending our last night in Boston with our dear friends Donna and Mike Eruzione. They had invited us to dine with them at a wonderful Italian restaurant, near the Charles River. We met Mike in 1980, when Suzanne and I directed the

Tangerine Bowl Parade and Half-Time Show in Orlando. We invited Mike to be the grand marshal of the parade. He'd become a celebrity overnight that year when he captained the U.S. Olympic Hockey Team that won the gold medal. We became friends during his stay in Orlando, and have remained close friends ever since.

The evening with Mike and Donna gave us a happy memory to take home from Boston. But, we still had to endure one more night in Motel Hell.

It wouldn't be the last time we were in Hell. No. Really. We would soon find ourselves in another Hell—Hell, Michigan.

We drove into Hell. There are so many jokes and puns here—but I'll leave that alone. It was hot, though—not kidding. We were on a two-lane road, and all we could see in Hell was a general store. We pulled in to get some snacks and directions to the haunted house we were to work on.

While paying for our food and drinks, I asked the woman behind the counter, who told me she was the owner, if there was more to Hell.

"This is it," was her clipped reply.

"Oh, really. Do you know where the haunted house is?"

Silence for a moment. Then she said, "You mean the tent?"

"I guess."

"It's up the road."

"Which way?"

She just stared at me, no hint of a smile. She pointed. We left.

In the car, we couldn't stop laughing. We found the haunted ... tent. We parked on gravel.

"Seriously?!" I said to Suzanne, as we climbed out of the car. I had been in haunted houses that consisted of wooden walls, constructed under a tent covering. That works. This was just a tent, with side flaps.

Suzanne just stared. "Good thing we got half our money up front."

My discussions with owners of haunted houses or hayrides—to design, work on, or paint in 3-D—were generally conducted over the phone, or by fax. The internet was not yet the tool it would become. Many times, I never met the owner until I began work on the job. I would send a contract, once we'd agreed on the work involved, and receive a first payment before work commenced. Sometimes, like now, we were not given the true details.

Suzanne and I walked up to the big, white tent. It stood on the edge of a dusty farm. There was dirt blowing as we stepped inside.

The farmer who had contracted me had told me the interior had a hard floor.

It wasn't hard. It wasn't a floor. It was sand!

The wind was blowing inside, through the billowing tent flaps, threatening to knock over the wooden cutouts that stood around the sides of the tent.

"Boy, am I glad this is a small job!" I said.

The farmer showed up. We introduced ourselves. I looked at the cutouts.

"Is this what you want me to paint?"

"Yup."

"To look like the flames of hell?"

"Yup."

I was having a hard time keeping a straight face. These plywood cutouts were no higher than two feet. When we had discussed this job, it was my understanding that hard panel, eight-foot high walls would be in place for me, on which I would paint 3-D flames. I had also sent him a sketch showing four-foot flames in front of those walls, and two-foot flames in front of the four-foot ones. He was supposed to make those cutouts for me. Now, a few two-foot high panels were all I had. Apparently, his vision of hell was quite different from mine.

"Is this all there is?"

"Yup."

I looked up. No black lights. Not that it would matter. There was bright sun and we were in a white tent. There was "no way in Hell" we were going to paint at night here.

"No black lights?"

"Not yet. Do you need them?"

"No. I'll be fine. We should be done by mid-afternoon."

"Okay." He left.

Suzanne looked worried. "Can we do this?"

"Sure. I'll paint two levels of flames on these panels."

"Okay."

And then the chickens came. We had blowing tent flaps in our faces, sand blowing on the wet paint, it was hot … and now, chickens!

Not two. A bunch. And they were nosy. They wouldn't leave us alone as they strutted around us and the paint.

It was a frustrating, long day, and, when we were done, paid (the farmer was thrilled with our work—go figure!), and we were finally driving off to another disappointing motel, I said to Suzanne, "That really is hell."

"Yes."

"Let's never come back here again."

CHAPTER 13
THE QUEEN IN LONG BEACH

The HMS *Queen Mary* had been a legend on the high seas until 1967. From her maiden voyage in 1936, this largest of the Cunard ships had ferried the rich and the famous back and forth across the Atlantic. During WWII, she was re-fitted and served as a troop ship, and dubbed the Grey Ghost for both her camouflage color and her speed, which was faster than enemy torpedoes. At the end of the war, she was returned to her former splendor as a passenger liner.

With jet travel making ocean liners less attractive, Cunard announced plans to sell the *Queen Mary*, and, in May of 1967, the city of Long Beach purchased the ship with plans to convert it to a floating hotel, tourist attraction, and maritime museum. Her permanent dock, on the bay in Long Beach, has given the *Queen* another career.

Suzanne and I had visited the *Queen Mary* as tourists more than once, and marveled at the beauty of this elegant ship. And now, we were going to "live aboard her" while we painted a 3-D haunted house.

Our boss, for this unique job, was Eric Prevratil, who'd contracted us at the Chicago convention show. We checked in and went to the stateroom suite he had reserved for us. This was like no other "hotel room" we had ever stayed in while working on a haunted house.

The art deco design and furnishings immediately took you back to the 1930s. The ship boasted fifty-six of the finest and rarest woods throughout its quarters, and several of them could be seen in our room. The bathroom had a huge tub, with the original dials for either hot and cold salt water or fresh water (the salt water was no longer available, but that option was representative of the detail that immersed you in the past). Of course, we had modern conveniences, such as a TV, phone, fridge, and air conditioning, but they were installed without harming the ambiance of the suite.

With our love of history, as well as art deco design, we were in heaven.

Eric met us at our suite after we'd unpacked, and took us down to the pier and into the temporary building there that would house one of the venues of Shipwreck, the name of the *Queen Mary's* Halloween attraction. He introduced us to Brian, who would be his assistant on this project, and our go-to person. We did a walk-through of the rooms, discussing what I would be painting in each as we looked over my sketches. The entire house would be in 3-D black light. He and Brian said they would have all my paints and supplies there the next morning.

We had the evening to ourselves, and we used it to explore more of the ship, including the promenade of shops and the views of Long Beach from the open deck.

The first big area I painted was the most fun for me because it involved an endless hallway, and in 3-D, that made it a favorite of the guests, too. It was constructed as four identical rooms, in a straight line, separated by a center opening in each. These openings had foam Gothic arches, which I painted to look like stone. In the last room was a wall in front of the guest, on which I painted the continuation of the hallway, in perspective, giving the impression that more rooms and arches were ahead. Many a guest walked into that wall!

Once they recovered, they realized the maze went to the left and into a jungle setting, complete with a bridge down the center of the walkway. This curved bridge, at its highest point only eighteen inches off the floor, spanned a river I had painted onto the floor. Using flat black paint, I created holes and broken planks on the bridge so the guests would try to jump over them. This room is where I perfected trees and vines, using the 3-D effect so that, as you walked through the room, these images appeared to shift and change as you moved past them. Numerous spiders hung from webs, snakes came down out of the trees, and creepy eyes looked out from the dark.

There was a jail scene and a Western town of skeleton cowboys. In that area was one of the best scares, involving an animated figure that shot out of the dark. It was a figure Eric had purchased at the convention show. It would not have been seen unless I painted it with black light paint, which I did—to Eric's smiling satisfaction.

One room we painted was actually a very long hallway, which began with black walls and floor. It required three separate layers of color, beginning with blue, painted as undulating, large squares on both the walls and the floor. When that dried, we painted the second level in green, overlapping the first squares. A third level was red. The worst part of this never-ending room was that, with each color, we had to do a base coat of white. The overall effect was a hit with the guests, but we vowed never to do this again! It took for … everrrrrrrrrr!! (All my idea—and a bad one!)

We worked long days—finished three rooms in the first two days—but we also had some chances to enjoy our stay on the *Queen Mary*.

One evening, our friends, Tony and Galena Cecere, joined us for dinner on the ship. Tony (previously introduced in the Sonny Acres chapter) was one of the foremost Hollywood stuntmen, known for his fire stunts. We were able to give them a tour of our work in progress, and it was as much fun for us as it was for them.

We were also able to take off time to attend a Rotary meeting in the grand salon of the ship. This room was the largest ever built on a passenger ship, at that time. It is three decks high, 143 feet long, and 118 feet wide. The woodwork, columns, murals, and décor are all breathtaking, and we felt transported back to a golden era just being in there!

We were sad to pack up and leave our suite at the end of ten days, but happy that Eric was pleased with my work. He indicated he would be asking us back again. That was something to look forward to.

And that's just what happened. We returned to the *Queen*; this time we were contracted to be there at least two weeks, and Eric reserved a larger suite for us. It just kept getting better!

Endless corridor at Shipwreck

HMS Queen Mary display of woods

Skeleton cowboy at Shipwreck

Snake in jungle at Shipwreck

Animated figure in Western town

CHAPTER 14
IN A WALNUT GROVE

The sun was shining. We were in California. The sun is always shining—usually. It was September 18, 2000, our 35th wedding anniversary. We had celebrated a day early, by going to Disneyland with our son Sean, Sande, and their friend, Cam. We always made it a point to visit Disneyland whenever we went to California.

Our next haunted attraction job was at a ranch in Moorpark, California, called Tierra Rejada. Because we had flown to California, and didn't have a car, Sean was our chauffer from L.A. to the ranch. Suzanne and I were to be house guests of the owners, Rick Brecunier and his wife, Linnea.

Our hosts made us feel at home right away. Their golden retriever, Boone, made friends with us the minute we got out of the car, and Sean played with him in the front yard for a few minutes before leaving. We immediately decided that Boone was the most relaxed dog we'd ever met.

Their home was lovely, and we were given a beautiful bedroom and bath suite. When they learned it was our wedding anniversary, they opened a bottle of wine, and we all toasted our special day as we got to know each other.

The following morning, Rick gave us a tour of the ranch, and showed us the haunted maze we'd be painting. It was in the middle of a beautiful walnut grove, and the maze was created by using old garage doors. It was almost complete. We watched as a fork lift moved another door into position.

Three workers stood the door up, connected it to the door beside it, and braced it at the back with two-by-fours.

Rick assured us that there would be areas ready for us to paint by afternoon. We talked further with him and Bill, who was overseeing the project, and we all felt confident that the maze could be finished on schedule. I asked additional questions, and pointed out where the black light fixtures should be mounted.

"That's a lot of garage doors, Rick! What gave you the idea to use them for a haunted maze?"

He laughed. "I have friends in construction, and when I asked them what used materials they could donate for this project, they told me about all these garage doors—and I thought, why not?"

"This will present some interesting surfaces to paint, but it should be fun. Great idea!"

By this time I was perfectly comfortable painting 3-D black-light figures in regular light, instinctively knowing how it would look under black light. In this case, I'd be painting under a canopy of walnut trees—in sunny California!

We only worked a couple of hours that day. Linnea had to attend a meeting that night, so Rick took us out to dinner; a great way for us to get better acquainted. Suzanne and I were already telling each other that this was going to be one of the most pleasant projects ever. And I was happy because there were no snakes, spiders, or rats—neither real, imaginary, or painted.

Next day, the weather was great, and we were painting a part of the maze themed around wizards. We finished that section, and I laid out, and Suzanne prepped, the next part of the maze.

That evening, Rick and Linnea treated us to dinner out again—this time at a delightful Mexican restaurant. We were joined by a neighbor couple of theirs. The dinner conversation was fun, and covered a variety of subjects. We got to learn more about Tierra Rejada, the ranch that Rick's family had owned since the 1930s. They told us that some movie stars had homes around the area, and that Walter Brennan, a favorite actor of ours from classic movie days, used to own the ranch next to them.

The Brecuniers and their friends were interested in our Disney careers, our family, and our involvement in theatre, among other topics. Since they'd met Sean, we shared our hope that he and his long-time girlfriend, Sande, might eventually marry.

"They could get married here, you know," Rick said.

"Here? Where?" I asked.

"In our walnut grove. We're getting quite a successful business, providing a venue for weddings and receptions."

"Cool! I'll tell them about it." Before we left the ranch, a couple of days later, we got to see them setting up for a wedding ceremony, in another part of the vast grove—and it was a beautiful setting.

Our third day of work saw the weather turn chilly, and Rick loaned Suzanne a sweatshirt to work in. We worked late, until about 9:30 at night, so we could get everything finished, except for line work on figures. It also allowed us to view the work under the recently installed black lights.

The long day had its moments of fun, thanks to Boone, the dog. We discovered he liked fruit when he stole an apple off our work cart, and lay near us, in the grass, munching away on it.

It wasn't until he was enjoying his bounty that I realized he'd purloined it from us. "Boone, that's not nice," I said. He finished the apple, looked at me, then brazenly strode over to the cart and took another one!

Suzanne and I both laughed, then I "hid" the rest of the apples from him, inside a secure container. Boone just watched, and continued munching the fruit.

On our last day, we awoke to a drizzling rain. What?! This is California. It never rains in California. Fortunately, the day was alternately sunny and cloudy, and the so-called rain didn't prevent us from finishing our work.

The Brecuniers had one more surprise for us. We took a three-hour break at midday, changed out of our paint clothes, and accompanied them to a Rotary luncheon held on top of a mountain nearby. It was actually part of a rock quarry owned by one of the Rotary members. Because Rick knew I was a Rotarian, we were warmly greeted by everyone. Lunch under tents, with such an incredible view, and great company, was a perfect way to finish our time on this job.

When Sean came to pick us up that evening, we took him on a tour of the maze, which he loved, and we stayed long enough to have a glass of wine with our hosts, who told Sean they were thrilled with our work.

Great fun, great people—great dog!

CHAPTER 15
HALLUCINATIONS- AND FANTASY

The stairway began at the floor, and proceeded in a geometric pattern upward, getting smaller and smaller as it progressed, leading to an open door where a shadowy figure stood. I had to wear 3-D glasses the entire time I was painting this illusion at the *Queen Mary*.

It was September, 2001, and Suzanne and I were back in Long Beach, for two weeks this time. Eric had us adding new effects to the house we'd done the year before. Those additions would only take a couple of days.

Before we began work on a new house on the pier, Eric wanted us to see the new Ghosts And Legends Tour, on the ship, which was a new tourist attraction for them. He wanted our advice, because of our Disney backgrounds, about how the Tour might be enhanced. I was thrilled, because now we were getting involved with real ghosts!

The HMS *Queen Mary* is famous for its haunted inhabitants, This was the basis for giving guests a guided tour of the frequent places where ghosts "appeared", including the indoor swimming pool, the bridge, the infirmary, and the engine rooms. Famous apparitions include "The Lady in White"; an unidentified young and beautiful woman, always seen in a white evening gown. She likes to dance in the Salon, and is frequently seen in various places on the ship from the lobby to the pool.

The last captain to sail the *Queen Mary*, and who brought her into Long Beach Harbor in 1967, is another of the frequent haunted sightings. His name was Capt. Treasure Jones, and he was fond of smoking cigars. The aroma of cigar smoke accompanies his ghostly image on the ship.

In 1966, a tragic accident, in Shaft Alley below decks, took the life of John Pedder, an 18-year old crewman. He was crushed and killed when caught in an automatic, steel door. He haunts that area of the ship to this day. Those are only three of the numerous ghosts that call the ship "home".

On the tour that day, we were below decks, in the bow of the ship, when the guide told us about the only serious accident the *Queen Mary* encountered during WWII. In October, 1942, while ferrying soldiers to England, and nearing the coastline of Scotland, the British cruiser, HMS *Curacoa*, cut across the bow of the Queen Mary.

The *Queen*, unable to maneuver away, sliced the ship in half. A large number of the *Curacoa's* crew died instantly, and their ship sank in less than five minutes. The *Queen Mary* could not stop to pick up survivors, because of the danger of U-boats in the water. She sent a radio message to other vessels in the area about the accident. With a gaping hole in her bow, the *Queen* made it safely to port. Some ghosts of the men who died have been seen in the bow area of the HMS *Queen Mary*.

Suzanne and I enjoyed the tour, even though we didn't see any real ghosts. We talked to Eric about our impressions of the tour, and I gave him some ideas I had about lighting and sound effects, and painting some additional images. Eric was enthusiastic about our coming back the following year to work on this attraction, but he was unable to secure the funds to do it. It would have been fun!

Years later (April, 2016), at a Zoo Crew/Entertainment Reunion in Orlando, we met with a former co-worker of Suzanne's; Patty Bender. She was the choreographer who had auditioned Suzanne when she was seeking her job in the Character department in 1978; a story Suzanne relates in our book, *Together in the Dream*.

We told Patty about that book, as well as the upcoming sequel, *Remembering the Magic*. But, it was when I brought up *The Design of Fear*, however, and my experiences with real ghosts – which I eventually did encounter—on the *Queen Mary*, that Patty delighted and excited me with her stories. We learned that she had helped create the Ghosts and Legends tour; the one we had toured, and which Eric had wanted us to enhance. Best of all, she had some great ghost stories of her own, while working on the Queen, and she was happy to allow me to share them in this chapter.

The year was 2000. Patty was working as an independent contractor with The Renaissance Entertainment Company who had been commissioned to create an attraction for the *Queen Mary*. The attraction would celebrate and illuminate the *Queen's* amazing supernatural history. It was to be titled Ghosts and Legends of the Queen Mary, and Renaissance re-created many of her most famous "hauntings". Patty served as producer for the film aspects of the production, and was the director on the install of the show.

Renaissance is a small company, and every production is "all hands on deck", so while Patty's title was producer as part of the small film crew, she was also craft services, costumer, casting agent and all-around "go-for-girl". The ship is huge, and filming was done at night. She was the only girl on a crew of five—which included one male actor.

Any time someone needed anything, it was Patty, with the weak, ancient ship's lighting and a hand torch, who clambered through the bowels of the ship. She was totally aware of the eerie creaks and groans down there. She felt like the only living creature that could hear those sounds. The only other noise she could imagine was that of a scream—her own—if she were to do so. Over the period of three nights, she had to crawl through a doorway, over a dozen times; one that had crushed a sailor – and where many have spotted his ghostly image. Patty swore she "felt him" every time she passed through that door!

Her personal ghost experience took place during the rehearsal period, after the film was completed. She returned to the ship, and was pleased to be given a lovely, small stateroom on the bay side of the ship. If you've ever been on a ship at night, you know it is incredibly dark – even at dock, if you're facing out to the ocean. No light seeps into a porthole, or even under a door. Consequently, Patty would sleep with the light on in the bathroom, with the door open just slightly to allow her to see if she needed to go in there during the night. One night, she distinctly heard her name whispered urgently in her ear. She opened her eyes, and, in the next instant, the globe light in the bathroom "exploded", leaving shattered glass on the floor, and Patty panting in the inky blackness of the stateroom. From then on, she says, she slept with her bible under her pillow!

She and her company rehearsed for a period of a few weeks, then had a big opening weekend during which the attraction ran continuously for twenty-four hours. They did exit interviews and heard some pretty fantastic stories of what people saw in the attraction, that weren't ones they'd created. The tour highlighted most of the well-known haunts of the *Queen Mary*, including the Woman in White, the sailor cut in half by the hatch, and the men killed when the ship collided with a smaller ship during World War II. It was impossible to recreate all the hauntings, but they did get rave reviews, and not just from the "fanatical fans" of the major stories.

During that opening weekend, Patty's parents, her mother's sister and her boyfriend (now her husband) happened to be visiting the area, so Patty took them through the attraction. Afterwards, they all went out to dinner and Patty asked her aunt what her favorite scene in the

Ghosts and Legends Tour was. She replied, "The little girl on the swing."

"Where did you see this little girl on the swing?" Patty asked her, puzzled because, though that is one of the many hauntings that's been sighted on the ship, it had not been recreated for this tour! Patty's aunt was seventy years old and a German war bride, and Patty knew she was not a fan of the *Queen Mary* and wouldn't have had a clue about the little girl ghost! She said she had everyone quickly return to the ship, she grabbed a video camera and asked her aunt to relive the "sighting". Unfortunately, the apparition was gone.

There was one more side note Patty shared with us. One of the owners of the company she worked for had moved to L.A. with her husband and 2-1/2 year old daughter. One weekend, the family took an outing on the Queen Mary. They were posing for a group photo, and her little girl wanted to make sure there was room for her new friend she'd just met on the ship. It was an invisible friend, but kids are impressionable, so they thought nothing of it.

When they got home, their dog began acting strangely, and their daughter continued talking to this "friend". Then, really spooky and increasingly malicious things started happening. For example, doors would slam shut and lock the mother out of the child's room, then magically swing open by themselves.

Of course, this being L.A., a psychic was easily found, and that person's theory was that a ghost had "attached" himself to the little girl, so they did a smudging and, thankfully, the ghost was never heard from again. Patty added that she was an associate producer on a movie, produced by Renaissance Entertainment, featuring those haunted pranks. The movie was called The Visitant.

I loved Patty's stories about her personal connections to the ghosts on the *Queen Mary*.

Now—back to work, on a new house on the pier, somewhat larger than the first one we did. It was to be called House of Hallucinations. This would contain an eclectic mix of rooms, including a dungeon scene, scary mummies, and what we called "the box room", a large area, with wooden boxes, from three-feet square to six-feet square, scattered throughout the room, and all painted in garish black light. The walls were painted with black light confetti and streamers. The boxes enabled the actors, dressed as clowns, to hide from the guests.

In the dungeon area, they had built a u-shaped cell that the guests had to walk around. An actor inside the cell would scream and try to reach the guests. I decided to paint each bar of the cell a different black light color, making it a repeating rainbow effect, so that the bars appeared to undulate in and out.

It took us more than a week to finish that house, and we were glad to move on, because this house had no air conditioning, making it uncomfortable on most days. Now, we were going to work in the geodesic dome, next to the ship.

This dome is the largest all-aluminum free-standing geodesic dome in the world, with a diameter of 415 feet, and a height of 130 feet. It had been built in 1980-82, to house the *Spruce Goose*, a prototype military transport plane built in the 1940's by billionaire Howard Hughes.

The Hughes Flying Boat, made mostly of birch wood—not spruce—had a wingspan of 320 feet, making it the largest aircraft in the world. The plane only flew once, on a test flight, with Hughes at the helm, in Long Beach Harbor. The flight lasted only one minute, and went one mile, flying only seventy feet above the water. The plane was installed in the Dome in 1982, as a tourist attraction. The plane was moved to the Evergreen Museum, near Portland, Oregon, in 1993.

Stepping into this huge, now nearly empty space, was overwhelming, to say the least. Eric led us on what seemed like a never-ending walk across the dome, to the perimeter of the building, which held offices and storage rooms. He opened a door, which revealed a 10-foot wide passageway, which followed the curvature of the dome. This was where Eric wanted us to paint a ninety-foot long mural on the slanting surface of this already curving room. This would make for some interesting, and sometimes uncomfortable, body positions while painting because we would be on a ladder, bending backwards.

The theme of this mural was fantasy, depicting everything from butterflies to zombies. You could call it my impression of somebody's strange nightmare; probably mine!

It took us long hours, and a week and one day to paint it, with evenings free to enjoy visits with Sean and Sande, as well as our friends Jeannie and Gerry Diez, who joined us for dinner one night. We also got to spend a Sunday at Disneyland with Sean and Sande. We were convinced, although Sean didn't say anything to us, that he was going to propose to Sande that day. It didn't happen, though.

In the end, Eric raved over our work. Joseph Prevratil, president of the *Queen Mary* (and Eric's father) complimented us with superlatives as well, when we met him late one evening as we were leaving the ship. He assured us that we would be invited back for future work. Very welcome praise indeed!

Staying that extra day meant that we were able to treat Sande and Sean to a celebratory dinner the night before we headed home. And what was the celebration about? Sean *did* propose *that* day, October 3, 2001, and, obviously Sande said, "yes"!

After our dinner, Sean surprised us by driving to Studio City. He knew I would really enjoy seeing actor Lou Costello's former home. (I'd always loved the movies he made with Bud Abbott; especially *Abbott and Costello meet Frankenstein*.) Sean couldn't have given me a better way to end our California trip!

As it turned out, we wouldn't return to the *Queen Mary* until 2003, because in the fall of 2002 we were home in historic Lexington, Virginia, for the wedding of Sande and Sean.

Disappearing stairway

Clowns and boxes in Hall of Hallucinations

Hall of Hallucinations facade

RJ and Suzanne painting curved fantasy maze

Celebrating Sean and Sande's engagement

CHAPTER 16
HEY, FRED, BRING A HAMMER!

I'm back in my home state of Illinois. Corn fields are fun places to run around in, when you're a kid; or even when you're an adult—but not in the middle of the night!

3:00 a.m.

It's chilly with a slight breeze. The hard-wall haunted house is covered by a tent. I can't imagine why anyone would want to come out to a cold haunted house, in the middle of nowhere. *Oh, wait—I'm here!—but that's because I'm being paid to create 3-D haunted rooms.*

It was the last room I had to paint, after seven days and nights. I was finishing a clown who was ripping through a wall. Guests, walking toward him while wearing their 3-D glasses, would experience his arms reaching out for them.

A loud crash. I jumped. "Who's there?"

Nothing.

Another sound; this one like something being dragged across the wooden floor, just outside the exit, where I kept my extra paint and supplies.

"Hello?"

The dragging sound stopped. I grabbed my hammer. "Hey, Fred!" I yelled, "Bring a hammer. Someone's at the exit!" Fred, my imaginary friend, did not answer. There was no Fred. I always called for "him" when I was alone, and scared of something unknown.

I slowly stepped out of the house to the entrance/exit area. "They're up here, Fred!" I yelled again, wishing there really was a Fred. I cautiously moved out from under the tent cover and looked around. I saw nothing. Lights lit the area just around the tent. I could see no human, no ghost. I almost laughed out loud. What the hell would a ghost, if that's what it was, be doing in the middle of a corn field?

A crunching sound to my right made chills run up my spine. I caught a glimpse of something, animal-like, disappearing into the cornstalks. Damn!

I did what I had to: hammer held high and screaming like a madman, I rushed toward the unseen thing!

I stopped at the edge of the lighted area. I listened. No sound. Probably a frightened rabbit, hiding in terror, thinking, "What the hell was that?"

Wait! Maybe it's a coyote! Shit! Or a bear!

Okay. Time to back up—quickly! I kept my eyes glued to the spot where I'd seen whatever it was disappear. Then I heard a sound behind me.

I jumped, and let out a yell. I turned around to see Bob's car pulling up. Bob was the owner of the attraction. I must have looked like a crazed maniac standing there, with the hammer raised above my head and a terrified look in my eyes. As Bob got out of his car, I lowered the hammer.

"You all right?" he asked, half-smiling.

"Yeah. I ... saw something." Pause. "Animal ... I think." Deep breath. "I need to get out of here."

Bob walked over toward me, as he scanned the corn field. "Big?"

"What?"

"The animal. Are you sure you're okay?"

"Yes. I don't know."

"You don't know if you're okay?"

"No. I mean ... it was medium size. Gray. And I'm ... fine. Sorry. I don't do well in the dark, in the middle of nowhere. Sounds. Rats. Snakes. It's...."

"Vietnam?" Bob knew of my past service during that war.

Long pause, before I answered, "Yeah. I'm okay." I led Bob into the house and dropped the hammer on the work table. "I just finished the last figure."

Bob put on 3-D glasses, and we walked through the black-lit rooms. There were no dark areas. No strobes. I hadn't been able to convince him to have areas like that, separating the rooms. But he loved it all, and that was all that counted.

He helped me pack my supplies in my car, and handed me my final payment. I waved goodbye and drove through the dark cornfield to the two-lane road that led into town. I breathed a sigh of relief, looking toward the lights of the town.

CHAPTER 17
BACK AND FORTH ON THE I-5

By 2003, the work at Del Mar Racetrack and the *Queen Mary* required all of August and September to complete. That meant I couldn't take on any smaller venues. Those two jobs were it, and they challenged me with their complexity.

Suzanne and I had no idea, when we started this, that we'd be travelling back and forth, from Del Mar to Long Beach to Hollywood to Pomona to Del Mar to Long ... you get the idea.

And I hate California freeways.

It began well. When we arrived at Sean and Sande's in Hollywood, it was early August, and Sean had a surprise for us.

"We've planned something different for tonight," Sean explained. "We have to go to the grocery store."

"Well, that's exciting," I said without much enthusiasm.

Sande rolled her eyes. "That isn't the surprise!"

"Okay, I take it you're not going to tell us anything else," Suzanne said.

"Well, if we did, there'd be no surprise, right, Mom?"

"Right."

With deli fried chicken, potato salad, cookies, and drinks, we were soon "somewhere." It only took about fifteen minutes to arrive at a parking venue in Hollywood.

Sean said, "Okay, now we have a short walk to your surprise. Have you figured it out yet?"

"Not a clue," I admitted. "Picnic in a park?"

"Close," said Sande. "We're eating our dinner in the Hollywood Bowl, and then watching a performance of *My Fair Lady* starring John Lithgow."

It was a perfect evening. Having a picnic, in our theatre seats—a tradition we learned, for those coming to the Bowl—as we watched the sun setting, was a great start to a wonderful, and unique, evening of theatre.

Next day, we journeyed to Del Mar to meet with Steve, and with Becky's assistant, Brandy. She was now going to oversee the Scream Zone project because Becky had been promoted, and would not be available on a daily basis. We did a walk-through of the attraction, and discussed changes and new areas. It was decided that we would begin work in two weeks.

On to the *Queen*, where we met Eric the following day, and did another walk-through. This one was to see the layout, in the geodesic dome, of the new haunted house that would be moved to the L. A. County Fairgrounds, in Pomona, once we finished it.

I said, "So, once we're done painting it, the crew dismantles it, takes it to the fair, and, when it's reassembled, we go out there and do whatever touch-ups are necessary. Right?"

"Correct," Eric replied.

"When does that happen?"

"You have seven days to get it done. It has to be out of the dome two days after that."

I just looked at him for a moment. He smiled. I couldn't believe I was smiling, too. "You're kidding, me, right? This is a 3,000 square foot house."

"Yes, it is."

I waited for him to say more, but, when he didn't, I asked, "Okay. I'll ask. Why the rush? When does the fair open?"

"It has nothing to do with that. A movie crew is coming to build sets for a major motion picture being filmed in here."

"Well, I guess we'd better go up to the suite and get into our paint clothes," I said to Suzanne.

During the years that we worked at the *Queen Mary*, three films used the dome for some of their scenes. The first was *A.I.* We saw Steven Spielberg arriving one morning, and Haley Joel Osmont playing just outside the dome one day. The second movie, *Pirates of the Caribbean*, used the building to construct the huge pirate ship, and film scenes on it. *The Haunting*, starring Liam Neeson, did some filming there as well—and left some props behind that we were able to use for one of the haunted houses. But we never got to see any of the actual filming when we were there. Damn!

Working on the Scare at the Fair meant ten-to-twelve hour days of painting and, once we returned to our suite every night, I was designing rooms for the next day's work. Again, Eric wanted room after room of 3-D themes, with no dark areas in between. We did a cemetery, a tropical creepy room, a room of ghosts, a shifting forest with wizards leaping out at you, plus he wanted me to paint another long hallway of overlapping geometric patterns, similar to what we'd done in the first house on the pier. *Oh, just shoot me now!* We did it, but we simplified it, because we didn't have a lot of time.

I have to give my wife some much-deserved praise here. Her part in all of these projects involved painting large blocks, or streamers, or circles, or outlined figures—whatever—with base coat colors and primers, so that I could do the design and detail work. I also taught her how to outline various areas. Her efforts saved me an immense amount of time, and she never complained about the tedium of her job (well, almost never!).

Eric knew we were giving the project our all, but that his deadline wasn't going to work. He gave us a two-day extension to complete the last rooms. Then, he instructed the construction crew to begin dismantling the rooms we'd completed. It made for a lot of noise—that dome caused lots of echoes!

The head of construction, John, and his able crew were a joy to work with. They never stopped commenting on my inventive designs; there was lots of joking and laughter, and a lot of Mexican music coming from their portable player. Each year, we looked forward to working with them all.

It was actually 3 a.m. on the tenth day when I finally finished this house. Suzanne had gone up to our stateroom hours earlier, because there was nothing left for her to do. I would have had a drink to celebrate, but the lounge was closed, and I was exhausted anyway.

The next morning, we checked out and went to Hollywood to visit Sean and Sande for a few days, before we had to start work in Del Mar. Eric called. He was so delighted with what I'd done, and so appreciative of the long hours it had cost us, that he offered us the suite for two additional days, just to relax and recuperate.

We drove back to Long Beach the next day, to take advantage of his "gift."

I did get my drink in the lounge after all.

After a restful couple of days we packed up again, got on the I-5, and headed south. Our first destination was Amy and Ray's new home, where we were to stay while they vacationed.

Brandy, the new person in charge at the Scream Zone, had an idea for one of the new rooms. She had seen this in another haunted house, but on a much smaller scale. It involved a platform, resting on hundreds of golf balls, so that as guests walked on it, it would shift in different directions. Steve and I were skeptical because Brandy wanted it to be placed in a 16-foot by 16-foot room. Our concern was that, in that large an area, the platform would be too heavy and too complex to construct and make safe. But, in the end, we gave it a shot.

A few days later, Brandy, Becky, Steve, and I were standing on the completed platform, laid on top of thousands of golf balls.

Becky looked at me. "Why doesn't it move?"

"It's too heavy," Steve explained. "When one person walks on it, they're not strong enough to make this huge floor shift, and the more people you add, everyone would have to move in the same direction at the same time, to make the floor shift at all."

Brandy was crushed. "Is there anything we can do to fix it?"

"Well, the truth is, we don't have time to mess with this room any further," said Becky.

"So, what are we going to do with this giant room?" Brandy asked.

I had an idea. "I'll do a Jackson Pollack!"

Steve laughed, and said, "What?"

"Pollack's paintings were just different colors thrown at, or dripped on, a canvas. I can do that to the surrounding walls and the floor. I'll begin with blue. When that dries, I'll paint wild skeletons in a battle with each other. Once all that is painted, I'll throw green on the walls, and red on top of that. This will make for a stupendous black-light room!"

Brandy's face lit up. "What if we also include a bubble machine to add to the room?"

Becky replied, "I like it all; let's do it."

As we were leaving the room, Becky asked, "What in the hell are we going to do with thousands of golf balls?"

To which I replied, with a grin, "Go golfing!"

We finished that room, and a couple of others, and when the weekend approached, Steve asked what we going to do with two days off.

"We're going to Disneyland!" I said, and added, "With Sean and Sande."

Steve stared at me. "Again?"

"Always. It's a family tradition—plus it's fun!"

We stayed two more days with Sean and Sande, because Eric needed to do touch-ups and an addition to the house at the Fairgrounds. It was so much fun, driving from

Hollywood to Pomona, and back again, two days in a row. It made no sense to stay at the *Queen* for those two days. We were already at Sande and Sean's apartment, which was about the same distance from the Fairgrounds as the *Queen Mary*. And, once we were done at the fair, we were going back to Delmar, for ten more days, to finish the Scream Zone. Needless to say, the I-5 route had become routine by this time, including the constant gridlock.

Our last days at Del Mar were spent creating a very strange maze, with painted suits of armor, drop-down panels for actors to scare guests, an alien room, and an eerie corn field.

I painted a corn field on all four walls, to give guests the impression that they were standing in the middle of it. The floor was painted to look like crushed corn stalks. As you walked into the room, you were facing the front half of an actual old car, with a skeleton behind the wheel. On a side wall, I painted a portion of a barn, and Steve built a split rail fence that attached to the barn and stood in front of the car—for guest safety. A sensor was tripped when the guest entered this room, causing the car to spring toward them, accompanied by the sounds of a roaring engine and a horn honking.

My last addition to this attraction was to paint a spooky forest on the main entrance wall into the barn, about 75 feet long. A fun way to end the year at Del Mar.

Becky and her staff were so thrilled with our work that they threw a party for us on the last day we were there. The staff, and even all the jockeys, grooms, vets, etc., in the surrounding barn areas; everyone made our work there a pleasure.

We didn't know then, but it would be our last work at the Del Mar Racetrack. In March of 2004, we were waiting in the lobby area of the Chicago convention facility, where the now gigantic Halloween show was going on, to meet with Brandy and discuss plans for their attraction. She called to say she was at a hospital ER, because her arm was painfully swollen. She suggested we call Becky, who was in a meeting in Chicago, to see if she could meet with us instead. That couldn't be arranged, but Becky said she would contact us when she got back to California.

Sadly, when she did call, it was with the tragic news that Brandy had succumbed to an infection that doctors were unable to stop. We were stunned. Becky explained that, because of this tragedy, and because she was too busy with other duties at the racetrack to oversee the Halloween attraction, the management had decided to contract with an outside company that would bring in their own pre-fab, haunted house.

We understood, but would miss working with the great staff and crew at Del Mar.

Back on the I-5—again—heading to Hollywood. When we arrived at Sande and Sean's apartment, we got a call from Eric—again. He wanted us to come back—again. I went to Long Beach and met with him. He had another haunted house, which he said would take about three days to do. Two days later, we were back in our suite, A155, on the *Queen Mary*.

This was an outdoor maze, with no roof. We would have to paint it in the daylight hours, because there was no artificial lighting there, and this maze had no black-light areas. We painted eighty-five panels the first day. The "theme" did not exist. It went from narrow alleys, to a Western section, to a swamp, to riverside shacks, and ended in a sandy cemetery. It was a last-minute addition, to help increase guest flow, and it was not a pleasant venue. There were bugs, spiders, and the ever-present sun. We were immensely happy to be done with it.

Finished with that, we checked out and went back to Hollywood to visit with our son and daughter-in-law before heading home. Then the phone rang. It was Eric. Could we come back for just a couple more days to do four new areas to the curved wall maze we'd done? And, he needed me to paint a sign for the outdoor maze.

"This will be quick," Eric insisted. "Two days, tops, I promise."

I laughed and said, "You'd better be right, because in three days, I will be heading east."

I finished the work for him at 9 p.m. on that second day. The extra money was good, the extra days I could have done without. Suzanne and I were both homesick.

At last, we were done with travelling up and down the coast of southern California, and were on our way home. While making our way back to Virginia, we had several serious talks about all the work we were doing in the Midwest and the West, and how we were only in our historic home half the year. Before we made it to Lexington, we had made the decision to sell our house and move to Chicago.

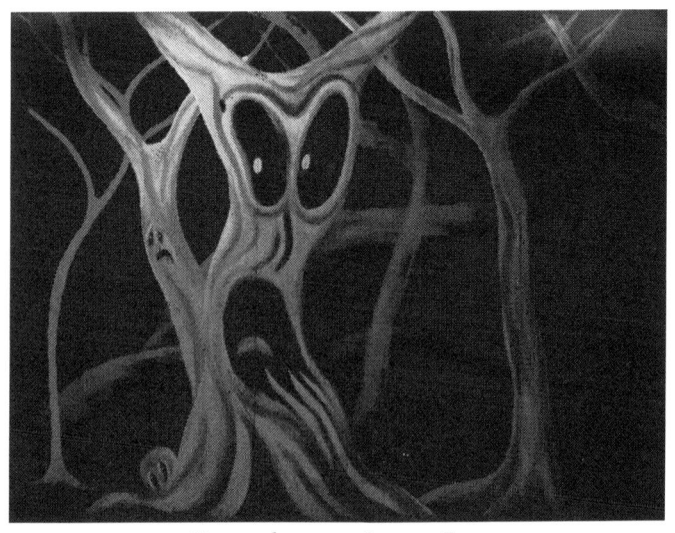

Haunted trees at Scream Zone

Shipwreck outdoor maze

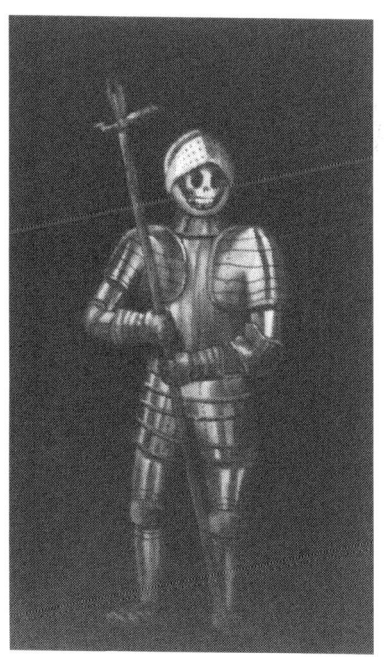

Skeleton night in Scream Zone

CHAPTER 18
PISSED-OFF PARROTS

In 2004, we purposely got to southern California a week before we were scheduled to begin work at the *Queen Mary* so that we could spend some uninterrupted time with our son and daughter-in-law in Hollywood. In the end, that turned out to be a good plan, because our work for Eric would be non-stop.

As we checked into our now familiar suite on the ship, it was nice to have employees welcoming us back, from front desk staff to servers in the lounges and restaurants. The next afternoon, I met with Eric to learn what our projects were going to be.

He gave me a detailed list. Topping it was a pirate-themed maze in the dome, the biggest maze yet. I was excited to begin drawings for that one. He wanted some changes to the Scare at the Fair (oh, crap, back to Pomona!), and he was also building a second haunted house, for the Fairgrounds, in a warehouse in L.A. We would paint it there and finish it off once it was installed at the fair. In addition, he wanted me to redo one of the houses on the pier, and make additions to two on the ship. We would end up working twenty-eight days, with only one day off—our wedding anniversary!

Our first day at the warehouse was a pleasant surprise. It was a fairly new building, air conditioned, with a full kitchen, a room to change clothes in, nice restrooms, and a huge area for the layout of the maze, giving us lots of room to work in.

Once we'd finished painting the rooms, and the house was disassembled and moved to the Fairgrounds, our "work conditions" disintegrated. The haunted attraction was re-assembled under the roof of a large picnic pavilion, near the edge of the Fairgrounds. We worked into the late evenings, it was cold (Eric had to find a sweatshirt for Suzanne to wear—which wasn't all that helpful), and it was a long walk to the restrooms. Eric was thrilled with the results; we were just tired!

On our 39th anniversary, we took the day off, beginning with breakfast from room service and ending with dinner at Sir Winston's, the premiere restaurant on the ship. We had a table by the glass wall of the restaurant, overlooking Long Beach Harbor, and two waiters to serve our every need. From the beef tenderloin to the Grand Marnier soufflé, everything was delicious. In addition, they brought us a chocolate cake for our anniversary.

I gave Suzanne an emerald and diamond necklace that evening, and she gifted me with an art deco wristwatch. It was the most extravagant anniversary gifts we'd ever been able to afford, owing to the sale of our Virginia home earlier in the year, and our move to Chicago. We continued our celebration with drinks and dancing in the Observation Lounge. Our favorite waitress, Christy, bought us a round as her anniversary gift to us.

This lounge had always been the best place to relax and unwind after a long day's work. The art deco design, coupled with the huge mural above the bar, created an ambience that was romantic and classy. Great drinks, great entertainment; sometimes a jazz quartet, other nights a great blues singer named Kat Tait (who also performed in Sir Winston's lounge sometimes), and even a really great Elvis impersonator one night a week. Whenever friends or family came to visit us on the ship, we made a point of having drinks with them there.

After our celebration, we were ready to paint pirates!

Pissed-off Parrots 119

The pirate maze gave me a chance to create ultra-dark areas, and became the favorite haunted house I'd ever designed. I created the artwork to tell a story as the guests walked through the attraction, wearing 3-D glasses. When they first entered the maze, they encountered pirates whose skin was just beginning to rot. In successive scenes, less flesh and more skeleton until, in the final scenes, they were completely skeletal with shredded clothing. The scenes progressed across an island, through trees, past a fort, in a dungeon, and on to a pirate ship, where they were in a hand-to-hand battle.

In one scene, I painted palm trees that faded into total darkness. As guests rounded a corner, the wall of a Spanish fort faded in. The dark spot was a perfect place for an actor to hide and scare the guests. In the fort, guests suddenly faced a skeletal pirate captain as he lit the fuse of a cannon. I painted a cannonball which would appear to come directly at the guests. Next, a hidden panel dropped down to reveal a rotting, pirate actor who would scream and reach for them, before disappearing back into the wall.

We worked very long days, and there were nights when I sent my wife to bed and continued to work alone, into the early morning hours. One of those nights, I was painting palm trees near the fort.

Darkness enveloped me as I moved through the shifting trees, rats peered out at me from the twisted tree roots and foliage. A loud, cavernous bang made me jump. I opened a hidden door, between two trees, and stepped out of the maze, into the huge geodesic dome.

Approaching footsteps echoed. The only light came from fixtures high up in the dome, making for an almost semi-dark atmosphere. I tried to peer into the distance, but saw nothing.

The footsteps stopped. I shivered.

"Is someone there?"

Nothing.

I moved slowly toward the sound, or where I thought the sound was coming from.

More footsteps, coming closer.

I still couldn't see anyone ... or anything. Why did I think this might be a "thing?" *There goes my imagination again!*

The footsteps had stopped once more.

"All right!" I shouted, "Not funny. Who's there? Eric?" Nothing.

Time for the old standby when I'm by myself. "Hey, Fred! Get out here! Bring a hammer!" I almost laughed out loud, as I thought, *Why is my imaginary friend always named Fred?*

Silence engulfed me.

Now the footsteps were close, but behind me. I jumped, and turned quickly. No one there! My breathing became ragged.

Then my fear rose when I realized it wasn't me breathing!

I whirled around. "Fred!" I attempted to shout, but my voice was weak. "Get out here now!"

Loud bang! A door slammed, on the far side of the dome, exactly where I'd heard the door earlier.

I ran back through the open maze door, grabbed a flashlight, and ran back out into the dome. Shining the light across the vast, empty space, I walked from the maze toward one side of the dome.

I glanced at my watch. It was four a.m.

I was alone.

All the doors were locked—weren't they?

I walked to a set of double doors and checked them. I even checked doors to storerooms and offices as I made my way around the dome. I spent nearly an hour checking the entire space. All the exterior doors were locked. During my inspection, I discovered, in some storage rooms, what was left of some aeronautical murals, which had been painted as backdrops to the *Spruce Goose*, when it was on exhibit there.

I looked back at the 3,000 square foot, pirate-haunted maze, sitting in the middle of the geodesic dome. It was dwarfed by the massive size of this space. I figured eight football fields could fit in here.

Finally, convinced I was really alone, I went back into the maze to continue painting palm trees.

At seven a.m., I opened a locked dome door and stepped out onto the pier. I was greeted by warm sunshine, the sound of seagulls, and the sight of the HMS *Queen Mary*. Spectacular!

In order to avoid guest areas, when Suzanne and I were in our spattered paint clothes, we entered and exited the ship from a gangway near the stern, an employee entrance that brought us to the back stairs, where we could ascend to the deck where our suite was, and, most times make it down the long passage to our room without meeting anyone.

Later that day, Suzanne and I were back at work creating pirates when Eric stopped by, and I told him about my late night experience with doors slamming, footsteps, and heavy breathing.

"It was ... scary."

Eric smiled. "Yeah. Some guy hanged himself in here, years ago. Numerous people have claimed to hear what you heard."

"Has anyone ever seen him?"

"Supposedly." He pointed to the curved ceiling, and walkway, far above us. "Hanging from up there."

"Charming."

All three of us looked up. Nobody hanging.

"I think I'll keep my eyes down here from now on," I said.

He laughed and nodded, then asked, "Did you figure out what to paint on the floor of the big room where the pirate ship is?"

"Yeah, I think you'll like it." We walked through a narrow, dark passage, and into a space that was larger than I would have liked. On the left side of the room, guests would get the impression that they were looking "down" into the bay at a pirate ship, at anchor, in the moonlight.

On the other walls of the room, I'd painted lots of trees, including palms and vines to give depth. I'd also painted two pirates, carrying a treasure chest and making their way through the scrub.

I had to come up with a way to keep the guests on a narrow path, in the center of the room. The solution was to paint flat stones, appearing to be in a large pond. Guests, would then "step" on the stones to get across the water. When Eric saw it, he said, "Yeah, this works. I like it."

"And now, for my favorite room!" I said to Eric.

"Is this the 'pissed off parrots' you keep telling me about? I just can't imagine scary parrots!"

"Well, just walk this way, and I'll convince you—I think."

Approaching the next room, I told Eric to put on his 3-D glasses before entering.

"Holy shit!" was his reaction when he stepped in.

Red, green, and blue, screaming parrots flew and twisted through an explosion of feathers which covered the walls and the floor. Two skeleton pirates swung at them with their cutlasses.

"When you said you were doing a parrot room, I wasn't excited at all. But this ... this is idiotic mayhem! What crazy nightmare caused you to come up with this? This is fantastic!"

"Remember what I told you the first time I tried to describe this room? I said, 'Think of these parrots as being held by the legs, smashed numerous times into the wall, and then let go.'"

I threw my hands up in the air, "Voila! Pissed off parrots!"

On our last day, Eric was unable to meet us to give us our final payment. Instead, his brother Robert—also an executive on the ship—met with us.

As he handed me my check, he said, "You've done, as usual, a fantastic job for us. And I have to tell you that my father, my brother, and I all consider you and Suzanne members of the *Queen Mary* family. We'll see you next year."

Hallway to our stateroom

Parrots and pirates in Shipwreck

Pirate maze guard

Pirates in lagoon room

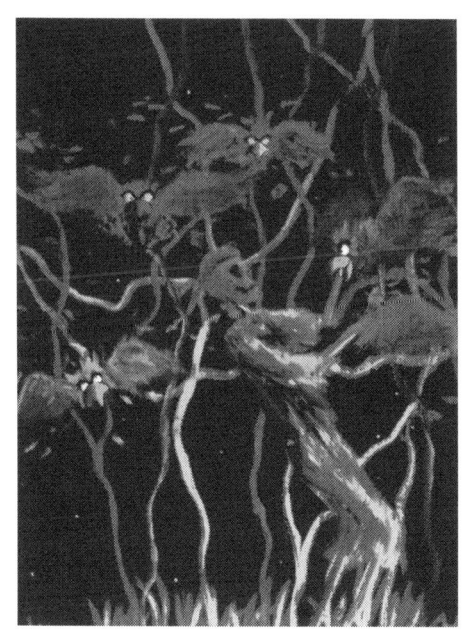

Pissed-off parrots

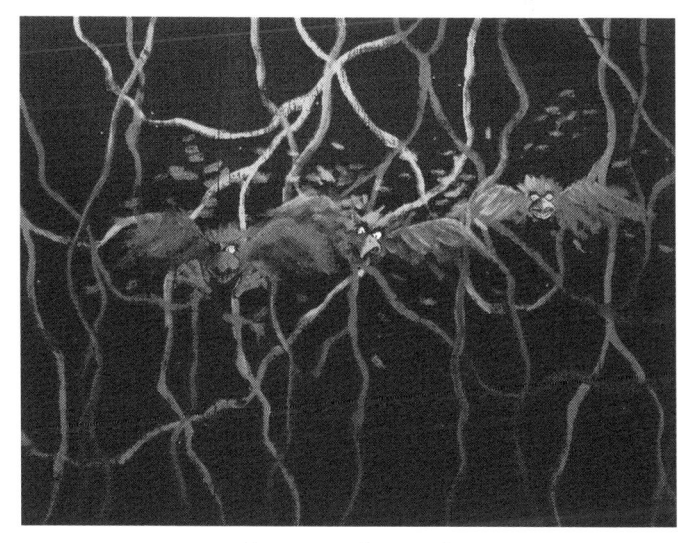

Parrots on the attack

CHAPTER 19
I DO BELIEVE IN GHOSTS

In March 2005, Eric and his assistant, Brian, came to Chicago to attend the annual Halloween convention, and Suzanne and I invited them to have dinner at our home. It was a rare chance for the four of us to socialize, it was great fun, and we finalized ideas for what we would be doing for Shipwreck in September and the beginning of October.

We decided to fly out to L.A. and rent a car there. This would eliminate almost a week of travel time, and we had grown tired of the long drive each year. It would also shorten the time our daughter, Dawn, would be responsible for our home and our dogs. She was a single mom with a full-time job and two small boys, Alex and Christopher, to raise.

Suzanne and I were met at the L.A. airport by Sean. Because we'd flown out there, we had a few days to spend with him and Sande before we had to start work at the *Queen Mary*. They surprised us with another trip to the Hollywood Bowl, this time to see John Williams and a symphony orchestra perform many of his compositions, including a *Star Wars* salute—another Disney connection there for us!

And, speaking of Disney connections, we had some with the *Queen Mary*, too, in a manner of speaking. First of all, Walt and his wife, Lillian, had been passengers on the *Queen Mary* during its heyday. (I have a picture of them, hanging in my studio, of the two of them on the deck of the ship.) There were many nights, after working long hours, that we'd take a stroll around the decks.

"I cannot do this without thinking I'm walking where Walt has walked," I'd say.

Suzanne would always smile and nod. One night she said to me, "Well, they talk about all the ghosts on this ship. Maybe he's still walking these decks—with you."

"Nah, he's at Disneyland." And there were nights when we stood on the stern and watched the Disneyland fireworks to the south.

The Disney Company had purchased the *Queen Mary* in 1988, with plans for a Port Disney resort and a theme park on the pier to be known as Disney Seas. The plans fell through in 1992, when Disney gave up their lease to focus on building what would become Disney's California Adventure. In December 1992, the *Queen Mary* was closed down. In February 1993, the RMS Foundation, with its president Joseph Prevratil at the helm, signed a lease with Long Beach as operators of the property. This was the company we worked for that came to refer to Suzanne and I as "part of the *Queen Mary* family." That, coupled with the Disney history of the ship, was very special to us.

By this time, we felt like family because employees of the ship knew us, and always made sure we had everything we needed as far as our work was concerned, but in addition, they took special care in other ways. A great example of that occurred a couple of days after we checked in.

Before we started our first work day in 2005, we went to the front desk to have some jewelry placed in a safe deposit box. One of our favorite employees, Veronica, took us into a room behind the front desk, and I placed the items in the box. Among these were a few treasured pieces that had belonged to Suzanne's mother.

Our day was busy. We did a walk-through of the attractions with Eric, met with him for a couple of hours, went off property to purchase supplies and food, and had dinner and drinks in the Observation Lounge. Back in our suite, I had just sat down at the writing desk to begin work on drawings for the additions to the haunted houses, when the phone rang.

Suzanne answered it. Her first response to the caller caught my attention, when she said, "No, it wasn't money. It was jewelry."

She hung up almost immediately, and said to me, "We have to go see Veronica. She found a fabric bag under the table, below the safe deposit boxes. I think it might be my mother's jewelry. Veronica wants us to come and identify it. She's been trying to reach us since noon." It was now after 7 p.m.

We rushed down there and met her at the door of the room behind the front desk area. She took us inside and asked Suzanne to describe what was in the bag. Once she did, Veronica produced the bag, and had me place it in our safe deposit box. It was then that she explained that she had discovered it shortly after we left that morning, and had put it in her own lock box until she could locate the proper owner. She had stayed two hours past the end of her shift until she could contact us. We couldn't stop thanking her, and later, Suzanne wrote a letter to Joseph Prevratil, praising Veronica and her extraordinary dedication.

Being alone, below decks, in the engine and boiler rooms, is unnerving. The spaces are massive, and there are constant sounds of running equipment, along with the pings and creaks associated with a ship, especially one built in the mid-1930s.

Scenes in the original *Poseidon Adventure* movie had been filmed in these spaces. I could envision Gene Hackman hanging onto a huge wheel-sized, shut-off valve, suspended near the overhead, thirty feet above the deck. His character was about to die. Probably not the best image to have in my head at the moment!

It was three in the morning, and I was working fast to finish painting more effects: illusions, spiders, their webs, and rats in this haunted space. There were three haunts for Halloween on the *Queen*—hey, nice rhyming! This one was called the Hull of Horrors.

I dipped my paint brush into the paint. A shadow crept across the metal deck I was kneeling on. The shadow darkened my hand. Startled, I jerked my hand back and looked up. A ghostly figure disappeared around the corner.

"Hello?" I gulped and stood up.

Footsteps.

Louder, I said, "Hello. Who's there?" I moved cautiously toward the sound, and peeked around the corner.

Nothing.

The metal floor stretched out before me; solid metal bulkheads on both sides. I could hear footsteps fading at the end of the passage, where it jogged to the right. I squinted, trying to see into the darkness.

Don't go there! It was the voice in my head insisting that I not do what people in scary movies always do; they go there! Stupid!

"You don't have to tell me twice!" I said out loud. I backed up slowly, but kept my eyes glued to the end of the passageway. I tripped over my paints and fell backwards; my right hand went into the red paint. Brushes and paint went everywhere!

"Damn it!" I sat there for a moment, looking at my blood-red hand. "Again?"

A loud clang, on the steel bulkhead beside me, made me jump up. I grabbed a rag to clean my hand as I looked around, but saw nothing. Again, I heard footsteps. And now, they were coming from below me, on a lower walkway. I looked over the metal railing next to me.

"Hey, you!" I yelled at the dark figure that was moving toward the stern. "This isn't funn...." My outburst faded, as did the figure. It had dissolved into thin air.

I gulped. "Oh, my God! It's ... it's a ghost!"

I was excited and frightened at the same time. "Wow!" I looked again to be sure the ghost was gone.

This had to be the ghost that so many people had seen below decks.

Seaman John Pedder had died when he was crushed by a closing hydraulic door as he tried to run through the opening, apparently on a dare. He was one of numerous ghosts that haunt the *Queen Mary*. He was not the only one I would see aboard the ship.

"I do believe in ghosts," I muttered as I cleaned up my work area, and went back to painting. "I do, I do!" My right hand kept shaking. "Damn!" *Maybe my left hand is okay.*

I can paint with both hands, a skill I worked hard to perfect, due to an injury I had in Vietnam, to my right hand.

No good; my left hand was shaking, too! "Bloody hell!"

Time to quit and go back to our stateroom, and get some sleep. I couldn't wait to tell Suzanne what I'd just been through. She woke up when I entered our stateroom suite.

"You okay?"

"No! Yes! I saw a ghost!"

"You what?"

I described every moment with the ghostly being to my wife. She was so tired, she asked if we could continue this discussion at breakfast, so she could go back to sleep.

The next morning, I admitted to her, "It's creepy down there. I don't know why Eric thinks I need to paint creepy images down there; it's creepy without them!" My wife agreed with me.

We both spent the morning, as we worked in that "haunted space," looking over our shoulders and jumping at the slightest sound. We were both quite happy to be done in the engine and boiler rooms.

Hull of Horrors below decks

Hull of Horrors on Queen Mary

CHAPTER 20
WORK, WORK, WORK— AND THEN FUN

After long hours of painting on the haunted attractions, or at the L.A. Fair, I would spend more hours in the evening, in our stateroom, doing sketches and color renderings for additions that Eric was requesting for the various venues.

I was finishing a room in Hallucinations, on the pier, and Eric walked in.

"I've got an idea."

"I hate when you start a conversation that way," I said, smiling.

He smiled back, but didn't hesitate to continue. "We're building a pizza stand and a photo location booth outside the dome. Could you sketch something you could paint on them that would look creepy?"

"Are these going to be in regular light or black light?"

"Regular."

"Yeah, I can do something. When do you need it?"

"Tomorrow."

"Of course you do." We both laughed.

We laughed because similar conversations had already happened between us, and I knew more were coming. This Halloween "attraction" had become huge. I now had three haunted houses on the pier, one in the dome, and three on the ship. Added to that were the three haunted venues at the L.A. Fair. We're not done! There were signs to be painted, small locations like the photo booth to paint inside and out, and there were three "big scares" I had designed that still had to be included in the pirate maze.

Good thing we weren't busy!

Work at the L.A. Fairgrounds alone involved a total week of work, but spread out over six weeks time. It was a 100-mile round trip from the ship to the fair; fifty miles one-way. Each work day resulted in long hours; one night we worked until 1 a.m., drove back to the ship, and were up at 5 a.m. to return.

The project at the fair that required me to be in the hot sun was also my favorite of everything I did there. It was the huge, menacing phantom I designed and painted for the front of the Scare at the Fair attraction.

Then, there was the last thing I did there, the night before the fair was to open; my least favorite (and it was cold that night!). Eric wanted a bloody-looking, directional sign for Scareplex. It was ten-feet high and twenty-feet long, on a rise at a junction of two paths. Because of the chilly weather, the paint wouldn't dry, and actually started running down the wood. I had to keep retouching areas, painting over others, and felt like I was in a haunted version of *Groundhog Day*. I didn't think I would ever be done with this damn sign! We were so glad when we finally left early in the morning, because the fair was opening later that day, and we knew we wouldn't have to go back to it anymore.

Every trip to Pomona also involved our having to pack all our supplies and paints into the car, and unload them at the fair, then do the opposite when we left each night. There was no secure location at the Fairgrounds to house them. And besides, the black light paint cost an average of $140.00 per gallon.

At least at the *Queen Mary*, we could lock the paints, etc., up in the dome. We had a cart that allowed us to move our supplies back and forth between venues on the pier. If we were working inside the ship, we had to carry whatever we needed to the site, and then take it back to the dome at night. It was exhausting as well as time-consuming, but necessary.

Eric came up with changes and additions to the outdoor maze, Trail of Terror, including more scares in the graveyard. Lastly, he wanted a few scares in the Hull of Horrors, requiring more 3-D black-light work. There was no work for Suzanne on that project, but she would keep me company as I painted. At least if a ghost appeared, I would have somebody with me.

This year, when we were working at the ship, we didn't have very many late nights, which allowed us to entertain family and friends who came to visit us on the *Queen Mary*. We even started early some days, so that we could stop work in mid-afternoon, giving us more time to spend with them.

Our good friends, Norm and Phyllis Koff, were in San Diego because Norm was attending a physician's seminar. They rented a car and drove up to Long Beach and stayed on the *Queen* so they could visit with us. We had known Norm since high school. He and Phyllis were both impressed with the ship, and all the delicious food we enjoyed while they were on board. I was touched by all their compliments of my work when we gave them a private tour of the haunted attractions.

About ten days later, Suzanne's cousin, Richard Rowe, and his wife, Carol, drove from Chino (where he had been city manager for many years), and checked in for one night on the ship. Richard treated us to dinner, then drinks at the Observation Lounge, then we all went to Sir Winston's Lounge, so they could enjoy Kat Tait's vocal talents. They were thrilled when we gave them a late-night, private tour of the pirate maze in the dome. Afterward, however, Carol said she would never go in there when the attraction was open to the public; too scary!

Sean and Sande got to see us more often than the year before, and we enjoyed that as much as they did. We spent one entire weekend at their apartment. We went to lunch with Sean another day. He was also able to provide us with some fun, because of his job. He was a manager of the Grove Theatre, a new venue that paid homage, with its architecture, to the grand movie theatres of the past. When we could schedule it, he was able to give us passes to films we wanted to see. In addition, one evening we joined him at the Paramount Studios for the screening of a movie. We were asked to comment on it afterwards, but the best part of that night was walking on the lot of that historic studio.

This would be the first year that Suzanne and I would still be at the *Queen Mary* when Shipwreck opened to the public. I was excited to see reactions from the guests enjoying my haunted creations.

Eric provided passes for Sean, Sande, and five of their friends to experience Shipwreck, and I accompanied them. Suzanne does not "do" haunted houses, once they are open, so she stayed in our stateroom. While touring the Hull of Horrors on the ship, they all commented on how they liked it, but were not frightened by the actors because they had no dark spaces to hide from the guests, then jump out and scare them. One clever actor did provide a great scare when he hid in the overhead of a passageway, and suddenly swung down in front of our group, while holding on to a pipe. Sean and Sande's favorite house was the pirate maze, and they all toured it three times.

We celebrated two anniversaries while we were there. The first was our 40th wedding anniversary, and again we dined at Sir Winston's, as we'd done the year before. We were pleasantly surprised when our waiter announced that Robert Prevratil had paid for our drinks and desserts as his anniversary gift to us.

The second anniversary had just as special a meaning for us. With Sean and Sande, we celebrated the 50th

anniversary year of Disneyland. We arrived when they opened that morning, and left after the fireworks late that night. One of my favorite moments was seeing the costumed character of Jiminy Cricket, the prototype of which I had designed at Walt Disney World in 1979. A lot of years had passed, and I certainly didn't expect to see it at Disneyland. (I told the amusing and detailed story about *my Jiminy* in *Together in the Dream*, available through Theme Park Press.)

40th anniversary dinner

Fright Mistresses' lair photo booth

Ghoul King at shipwreck

Hall of Hallucinations ghostly figure

Pizza Shack

CHAPTER 21
THE MAW

My wife and I were busy inside the dome, finishing the last of my big scares for the pirate maze, when we heard an unusual sound (for California): rain on the roof. In a little while, we could hear water splashing onto the concrete floor of this giant building. We stopped painting and stepped outside the maze. Rain water was coming through several places in the roof; luckily, none of the water was leaking into the maze itself. I called Maintenance and they sent someone to put buckets down where the leaks were. Good thing it wasn't raining really hard.

Rain leaks were not much of a distracting noise to us. On several days a week, though, there was noise of a different kind that was annoying. Recently, Carnival Cruise Lines had leased half the area of the dome to function as their arrival and departure terminal, for their cruise ships that left from Long Beach. A thirty-foot wall had been built that split the dome in half physically, and separated us from that area.

Because of the echoing nature of the dome, the crowd noise in the terminal reverberated all over the place. At times, we could even pick up individual conversations. Adding to that cacophony were the announcements over their public address system. We were always happy when there were no Carnival ships in port.

One morning, near the end of our stay on the *Queen Mary*, as we were heading to the dome, I noticed a young man demonstrating a Segway on the promenade leading to the Carnival terminal. We walked over to watch the tourists trying out the Segway, which was new at the time, and people were excited about it—one of those people was me. The demonstrator gave me some brief instruction, and I got to take a five-minute ride—the first two-minutes of which were extremely erratic, and hysterical to Suzanne!

Back on solid ground, we were focused on completing the last of the scares for the pirate maze. The first of these was in a dark passageway, which included a sharp right, then left turn. Guests would be chased through there by a pirate actor. I wanted to put something on the floor that would cause them to stop dead in their tracks before they realized they could not get away from the actor without running over this terrifying creature. And what was this terrifying creature, you ask?

I'm not going to tell you! Just kidding; it was a twelve-foot, mouth-agape alligator, "swimming" toward the guests. With their 3-D glasses on, his huge, toothy jaws would appear to be rising up from the floor, ready to chomp down on them. To my delight, it worked like a dream.

The second scare involved a stable of bloody, almost rabid-looking horses, whose 3-D images followed the guests as they moved past the stalls. Most of the colors in this room involved reds, oranges, and blues. I love horses, but these images were sick—even if I did paint them that way.

I saved the best for last, as they say. Near the end of the maze, one large room had been split in two. When you entered the first room, there was a wall in front of you, with a four-foot by eight-foot wide opening in the center, which led into the second room. I told Eric that I wanted the first room to be lit by black light, and the second to be totally dark. Not being a fan of dark spaces, Eric wanted black light in both spaces, but I convinced him to let me paint the image I wanted to do in the first room, before he decided on the second room. This was the only time I didn't give him a sketch of my idea; I wanted this to be a complete surprise. He reluctantly agreed, and I set to work.

The next morning, Eric and Brian came into the dome. I stopped them and gave them 3-D glasses, then had them enter the first of these two rooms.

"Holy crap!" yelled Brian, as Eric screamed, "Wow! I never expected this!"

Before them, painted around the opening, loomed a nine-foot high head of a skeleton, its eyes glaring down at them as it opened its immense mouth. Its lower teeth and chin were painted onto the floor. With the second room totally dark, it made the area past the mouth, and beyond, a place no one wanted to venture into. Going into the unknown was as scary as the "maw" they had to pass through. I'd finally made a believer out of Eric about dark spaces!

Alligator in maze

Creepy horse in pirate maze

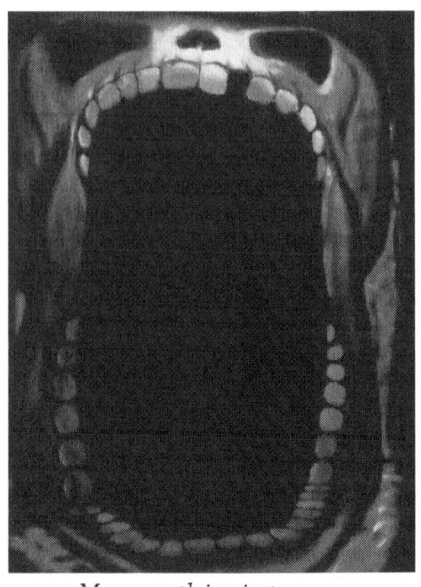

Maw mouth in pirate maze

CHAPTER 22
...AND BEYOND

We couldn't have known, when we finally said goodbye to all our friends and co-workers in October of 2005, that it would be our last year to enjoy such a remarkable experience in Long Beach. Another company would take over the ship in the following few months, and they would hire other people to oversee the Halloween venues. Suzanne and I would miss our annual fall stay, in that beautiful stateroom, aboard the HMS *Queen Mary*.

I certainly haven't been idle since 2005. I continue to do paintings and murals on commission. I recently completed one of my largest murals in Wheaton, Illinois, entitled Pearls of the Universe; it covers a 70-foot by 23-foot outdoor wall. It shows the diversity of Wheaton's citizens, and their journeys to America.

At the Chicago Museum of Science and Industry, I created pixie dust swirls across 150 feet of wall space, for the entrance into the exhibit entitled Treasures of the Walt Disney Archives. The pixie dust was lit by black light—can't get away from it!

I've designed and painted sets for numerous theatres in the Chicago area, but recently, the bulk of my scenic design and scenic art has been for Playhouse 111 in Wheaton. One of those sets, for their production of *Into the Woods*, was done in both regular stage lighting and in black light.

The past two summers, I've spent many weeks in Lake Geneva, Wisconsin, designing and creating venues for a mini-theme park, Dancing Horses. I was originally contracted to design and update their arena horse show, and I created one of the sets for that show in black light. I have gone on to design and paint other exteriors there, including an Indian tepee village, a baby animal barn, an outdoor petting zoo area, and the front of the arena theatre. In a separate project, the owner had me design, supervise construction of, and paint a pet resort named LolliPups.

My most recent black light creation, Escape for Fun, is an escape room entertainment venue in Wheaton, Illinois. The design is based on a castle setting and a dungeon. Groups of up to ten people are locked inside the escape room, with sixty minutes to solve the clues inside and unlock the exit door.

I'm currently working on illustrations for two different children's books (no black light in these), for two different authors.

A lot of my time now is divided between books I'm writing or promoting. *Together in the Dream: the Unique Careers of a Husband and Wife in the Early Decades of Walt Disney World*, co-authored with my wife, Suzanne, is available through Theme Park Press. A sequel to that book will be published in the near future. We are also doing speaking engagements, either about our Disney experiences or with a motivational theme about pursuing your dreams. We both know they can come true!

Suzanne and I aren't always working, although sometimes it seems that way. At the end of our book, *Together in the Dream*, written just before we were going to celebrate our 50th wedding anniversary, we said we would be celebrating our milestone at Walt Disney World. And we did! For a glorious week, we both relived memories, and made new ones, in the place where it all started.

On our first day at the Magic Kingdom, we rode in my favorite black-light ride, Peter Pan's Flight. Our last night at WDW, we were back in the Magic Kingdom, and, just before leaving, we visited my favorite haunted house (for the second time!): The Haunted Mansion. We hadn't planned it that way, but it was the perfect way to end that special week—and it's the perfect way to end this book.

50th anniversary dinner

Dancing Horses black light set

Escape for Fun dungeon

Escape for Fun dungeon entrance

Escape for Fun entry room

Museum of Science and Industry pixie dust

LolliPups entrance

LolliPups kennel entrance

Indian Village

Painting teepees in Indian Village

ACKNOWLEDGMENTS

To my publisher, Bob McLain, who encouraged the writing of this book, and to my wife, Suzanne, who then helped me tell the story because she lived it with me.

To Jim Feltes, and family, of Sonny Acres; to Rick and Linnea Brecunier of Tierra Rejada Ranch; to Becky Bartling of Del Mar Racetrack; and to Eric Prevratil and his family on the *Queen Mary*. They all gave me extraordinary opportunities to stretch my creativity. In addition, I must thank the many, many people who helped in the construction, lighting, and special effects of all the haunted attractions I tell about in these pages. I wish I could name you all individually.

At Walt Disney World, I worked with so many creative and talented people. I will always be grateful for the opportunity, and for all the knowledge I gained there as a result. I must mention the three artists who worked with me every day in the Magic Kingdom: Lee Nesler, Tom Rodowsky, and Jayne Polgar. I think of us as "the fabulous four."

Lastly, to my family and friends, your support and never-failing belief in me keep me always moving forward to my next creation. There are not enough words to express my thanks for that.

ABOUT THE AUTHOR

R.J. Ogren is a former Walt Disney World management audio-animatronic artist who painted all the attraction figures, murals, and props at the Magic Kingdom in the 1970s. He has had a varied and successful career as a freelance artist, scenic artist, writer, illustrator, and guest speaker. He lives near Chicago, with his wife, Suzanne. They co-authored, *Together in the Dream* available through Theme Park Press. His website is rjogren.com.

More Books from Theme Park Press

Theme Park Press is the largest independent publisher of Disney, Disney-related, and general interest theme park books in the world, with dozens of new releases each year.

Our authors include Disney historians like Jim Korkis and Didier Ghez, Disney animators and artists like Mel Shaw and Eric Larson, and such Disney notables as Van France, Tom Nabbe, and Bill "Sully" Sullivan, as well as many promising first-time authors.

We're always looking for new talent.

In March 2016, we published our 100th title. For a complete catalog, including book descriptions and excerpts, please visit:

ThemeParkPress.com

Our Careers in the Magic Kingdom

R.J. painted animatronic figures and "plussed" attractions. Suzanne drove monorails, marched in parades, and entertained as Sleepy the dwarf. Together, the Ogrens brought their unique skills to Walt Disney World's Magic Kingdom during its formative years.

themeparkpress.com/books/together-dream.htm

The Rosetta Stone of Disney Magic

Warning! There be secrets ahead. Disney secrets. Mickey doesn't want you to know how the magic is made, but Jim Korkis knows, and if you read Jim's book, you'll know, too. Put the kids to bed. Pull those curtains. Power down that iPhone. Let's keep this just between us...

themeparkpress.com/books/secret-stories-disney-world.htm

Welcome, Foolish Readers

Haunted Mansion expert Jeff Baham recounts the colorful, chilling history of the Mansion and pulls back the shroud on its darkest secrets in this definitive book about Disney's most ghoulish attraction.

themeparkpress.com/books/haunted-mansion.htm

Who's Killing Cast Members

In this debut novel from former Disney World VIP Tour Guide Annie Salisbury, a body has turned up in the waters of the Jungle Cruise. Wrongfully accused Cast Member Josh Bates must race through the theme parks to solve the murderer's maddening riddles and clear his name.

themeparkpress.com/books/murder-magic.htm

Disney the World Over

Clemson University professor Stephanie Barczewski delivers a scholarly but accessible comparative history of the Disney theme parks, from Anaheim to Shanghai, with a focus on the engineering, cultural, and political challenges that Disney overcame to build its "happiest places" across the globe.

themeparkpress.com/books/magic-kingdoms.htm

Terrifyingly Updated for 2016

Stakes? Check. Silver bullets? Check. Survival guide? If you're brave enough to attend Universal Orlando's Halloween Horror Nights, you better believe you'll need a survival guide. Complete with a detailed history of the event, this book is all that stands between you and *them*..

themeparkpress.com/books/halloween-horror-nights.htm

Printed in Great Britain
by Amazon